IMAGES
of America

FORT WRIGHT

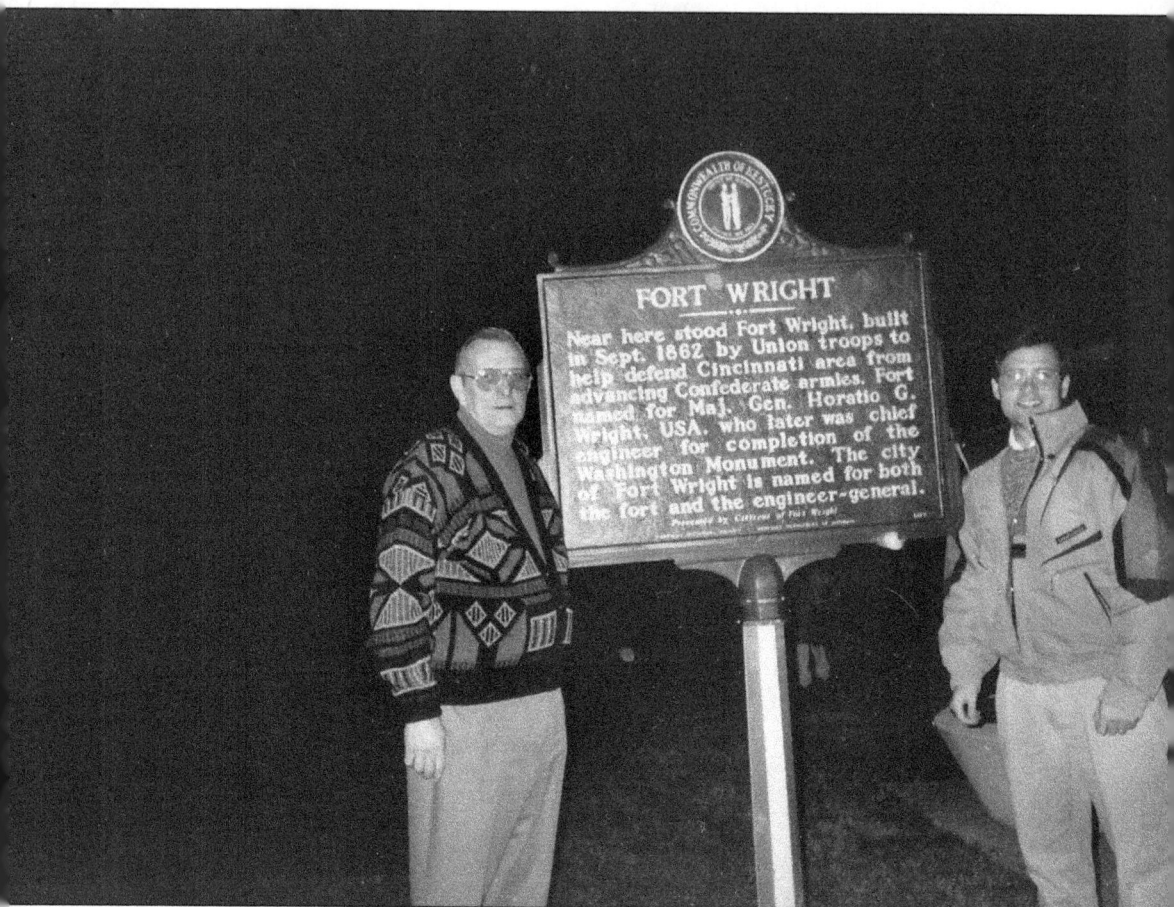

Don Martin Sr. (left), Don Martin Jr., and family led efforts to place this historical marker at Fort Wright City Hall. It reads in part, "Near here stood Fort Wright, built in Sept. 1862 to defend Cincinnati from advancing Confederates." The city is named for that fort and commander Gen. Horatio Wright. Martin Sr. served the city as mayor, councilman, police judge, police officer, fireman, and more. (Courtesy of the Fort Wright Fire Department.)

ON THE COVER: The August 16, 1957, *Kentucky Star Times* said firemen extinguished a fire at Shilling's Restaurant, 1939 Dixie Highway, Fort Wright. The grill blaze spread up a grease vent to the roof. Pictured from left to right, Fort Wright firemen George Kreutzjans Jr., Bill Janszen, and Roy Hoppenjans chopped a hole in the roof to put out the flames. (Courtesy of Don Martin Jr.)

IMAGES
of America

FORT WRIGHT

Julia Hurst

ARCADIA
PUBLISHING

Published by Arcadia Publishing
Charleston, South Carolina

Library of Congress Control Number: 2009922407

For all general information contact Arcadia Publishing at:
Telephone 843-853-2070
Fax 843-853-0044
E-mail sales@arcadiapublishing.com
For customer service and orders:
Toll-Free 1-888-313-2665

Visit us on the Internet at www.arcadiapublishing.com

I dedicate my first book to my parents, husband, and children who make putting one foot in front of the other every day both possible and glorious

CONTENTS

ACKNOWLEDGMENTS

As with all things in Fort Wright, this book is only possible as a result of neighbors helping neighbors. I deeply thank the courtesy of each person and group listed here for sharing support, knowledge, and photographs for this book to help showcase that Fort Wright is the City of Cities: specialist Dean Russell; fire chief Steve Schewe; Don Martin Jr.; Jack and Charlotte Nienaber; Joseph Sr. and Peggy Nienaber; the Kenton County Library in Covington, Kentucky, an outstanding regional asset every Northern Kentuckian should value; Joe Averdick; Nick and Cyrilla Brake; Bob Clements; the City of Fort Wright and its staff; the Diocese of Covington and archivist Thomas Ward; the Drees Company; Frances Emark; Adam Feinauer; Finke's Meats; Joe Fischer; Fort Wright Civic Club and the Hilltopper Club; the Gilliam family; Dave Hatter; Barbara Hellmann; Tom Hoppenjans; Julia and Debbie Kremer; Gerry Kreutzjans; Clarence Lassester; Phillip Landwehr; Lookout Heights Civic Club; Bill Nienaber; Mayor Joseph Jr. Nienaber and Holly Nienaber; Bernie Spencer, Northern Kentucky Views; Bob Ratermann; Kathleen Romero; St. Agnes Church and Fr. Mark Keene; Katie Scheper; Roger Scwartz; Donna Sheehy; Ann and Dave Stutler; Marianne, Kevin, and Scott Wall; Bernie Wessels; Allan and Betty White; Katie Wolnitzek; Bob and Helen Zembrodt. And others who contributed to the city's collection: Nancy Oelsner Baute; Rose Helen Bowling; Mary DeSalvo; the Foltz family; Roy and Laura Hoppenjans; Martha Kuchle; John McCormack; Jack Murphy; the Siegrist family; Harry Schwabe; Tom Stamm; Carol Whitehead; Roy Willer.

Thanks to Arcadia Publishing for giving Fort Wright and me this chance. Thanks to Regan Coomer, the *Recorder* newspaper, and the *Kentucky Enquirer* for helping neighbors connect through their coverage of the writing of the book. I offer sincere apology for any omission or error.

I thank the immediate and extended members of the Lohmeier and Nienaber families for teaching me the value of faith, family, hard work, responsibility, public service, and living the dream. Above all, I thank God from whom all blessings flow.

INTRODUCTION

In looking over the more than 600 photos, videos, maps, and collections lent for this book, I asked my six-year-old son, "What makes Fort Wright beautiful?" He pushed his glasses up his nose, sat up straight in his chair, fingered over the collection, and smiled. "It's that everyone says hi to us when we walk around the block!"

From the mouths of babes.

Fort Wright has what every community must, with solid homes, many of good German construction, established police and fire protection, a public and private school, an active business community, an engaged citizenry, and spiritual opportunities. And Fort Wright has more: a storied history, unmatched resident initiative, and an unparalleled location traversed by nearly every major thoroughfare in the region.

The hallmark, though, of every chapter of the Fort Wright story is its people, the families who have stayed and the individuals who have soared to build the city's foundation. "While cities provide infrastructure, safety, equipment and order, the true value of Fort Wright is in its people. Fort Wright has been rich with civic, political, religious, and social leaders —as fathers, coaches, neighbors, volunteer firefighters, parishioners, and friends," said Mayor Joseph Nienaber Jr. in November 2008.

Fort Wright is the City of Cities, with a history of neighbors helping neighbors that could become the stuff of legend. In 1862, thousands of neighbors heeded the call to build a defense, nearly overnight, to protect Cincinnati from Civil War raiders. In 1950, forty Fort Wright men volunteered to become firefighters. In 1952, the Bob Meyers family would forego a home being built so Nikolaus and Marie Kreutzjans, recent immigrants, could occupy the house. In turn, through the years, the Kreutzjans would board other immigrants in that same home. When Kentucky suspended public kindergarten education, Betty White answered the community need by educating 450 children over 19 years in her Fort Wright home. In its history, Fort Wright neighbors would band to form three civic clubs and a private swim club within its 3.5 square miles.

Fort Wright was the site of legions of defense for Cincinnati in 1862, when Confederates threatened to raid. One of the thousands of volunteers was Lt. James Martin. His descendents remain in Fort Wright today. James is the great-grandfather of Don Martin Sr., Fort Wright mayor from 1989 to 1993. Don Martin Jr. is a veteran of nearly 20 years from the volunteer fire department, and he served on city council. The Martin family worked to get a historical site marker and veterans' memorial placed at today's Fort Wright City Hall. The historical marker notes the city's role in defending Cincinnati from Confederates.

In the 1800s, Fort Wright was largely rural farmland. An 1820 deed indicates the "old homestead" had been built on today's Augusta Avenue. In 1834, the Covington and Lexington Turnpike Road Company was chartered to build artificial roads, and toll roads were in force in Kenton County until 1912. In 1850, the macadamized road of the Lexington Turnpike (Dixie Highway) was completed. The Robert Kyle homestead and farm was used in the 1862 Civil War defense.

Today's Kyles Lane is the namesake of Robert Kyle. In 1832, on the Banklick Turnpike (Madison Pike or 3-L Highway), the Latonia Springs Hotel was built and owned by a doctor as a mineral water spa.

In the 1900s, the area remained rural but the turnpikes grew. Within what would become the city, the Foltz family farmed vegetables, the Henry Knochelman farm was established, and famous area surgeon Dr. Charles Pieck built a country residence. The Kuchle family built a homestead and at the Lexington Turnpike and Kyles Lane. In 1886, a cupola, the Lookout, was built from the former Rush's Tavern. In 1912, Bill Hill bought the Lookout and its popularity grew. On Banklick Turnpike, the Latonia Ice and Fuel Company harvested ice from Mueller Lake, an important task in this era before electric refrigeration. The Holy Guardian Angel Church was built in 1880 and a school opened in 1909. August Ratermann and Herman Summe bought the former Latonia Springs Hotel land in around 1891 and made a dairy farm. And the profitable goldfish breeding industry prospered across the city.

Perhaps the largest development of the new century was the automobile. In 1901, automobiles were seen as a luxury for the wealthy, and few automobiles traveled Fort Wright roads. But more than 240 automobile manufacturing firms started business in the United States between 1904 and 1908, according to CNET News. By 1920, Ford had sold more than one million cars. Travel was slowly shifting from foot, horse, streetcar, or bus to the personal automobile. This significant cultural and economic shift impacted the development of Fort Wright business on both turnpikes and was a consideration of Fort Wright's earliest residential developer.

In 1922, the Kuchle blacksmith shop on Lexington Turnpike was converted and opened as an automobile garage. From 1924 to 1928, Dixie Highway was under construction, so all through traffic to Lexington and Louisville used Madison Pike. Madison Pike thrived with booming gas stations, barbecue stands, vegetable stands, and cafés. The *Kentucky Post* reported as many as 1,000 automobiles per day passed through at the height of tourist season. Latonia Springs Picnic Grounds and Camp was busy on Madison Pike, partly from Latonia Racetrack business. When construction on Dixie Highway was complete, the U.S. Highway Commission returned the Route 25 designation to it, and Madison Pike traffic slowed dramatically, crippling some businesses.

With Dixie Highway complete and traffic returned, business flourished. The St. Agnes Chapel and School opened on land that previously was the Henry Knochelman farm. The Lookout House anchored the Gourmet Strip, which included Oelsner's and Jack's Tavern in what would become Fort Wright. Residential development started occurring around the area. The Heart's Desire development opened in 1927 in South Hills, and Lookout Heights incorporated in 1937. In 1938, St. Agnes built the church much as it looks today.

In 1937, George Kreutzjans Sr., Theodore Drees, and Henry Knochelman agreed for Kreutzjans and Drees to build residential homes on Fort Wright's earliest streets, the Edna Lane and Crittenden Avenue area. The $5,500–$6,500 houses were generally brick, one-and-a-half-story Cape Cods with two bedrooms, a kitchen, living room, and bath. The homes were solid, functional, and comfortable with an upstairs that could be finished as families grew. Since many people then could not afford both a car and a house payment, the developers worked with the South Hills Heart's Desire developer to get public bus service to the area. After finishing the Knochelman lots, Kreutzjans and Drees purchased land from Mr. Rehkamp, a local dairy farmer. In 1940, the partnership dissolved amicably, leaving Kreutzjans to develop Fort Wright. Kreutzjans, an immigrant from the small town of Lorup, Germany, would become the father of Fort Wright.

In 1941, the neighbors of Fort Wright began meeting in each other's basements regarding the affairs of the area. The Fort Wright Civic Club was formed and the City of Fort Wright was incorporated. During these early years, the civic club paid for all city debt and street repairs. The civic club was responsible for conducting most municipal affairs. Door-to-door city mail service was instituted on July 1, 1941. In 1944, due to war and defense work, the civic club was in a bad state. A letter that referred to the dark before the dawn was sent to all members, asking if they wished to disband. By 1946, civic club meetings were so large that they no longer fit in basements. A clubhouse was erected, and the cost of constructing the building was paid off in two years.

The impact of greater automobile ownership and interest continued to be felt in the city. A streetcar that charged a nickel per pass was still running from Fort Mitchell, through Fort Wright and Park Hills to Covington. But more people owned and were driving automobiles, too. On Dixie Highway, Kuchle Garage opened an auto showroom in 1946. The Dixie Gardens drive-in movie theater opened in Fort Wright in 1947, one of the first in Northern Kentucky. The Ratermann land on Madison Pike, the former site of a hotel and later dairy, was now Latonia Auto Salvage. By 1950, the salvage yard had a selection of 2,000 automobiles.

The dawn of the new decade in 1950 again brought great change to Fort Wright. In 1949, neighboring South Hills incorporated. In Fort Wright, a need for fire protection was determined, and about 40 volunteers began training as firemen. In 1950, the Fort Wright Volunteer Fire Department organized, and in May, the first piece of firefighting equipment arrived. In 1951, a state raid of the Lookout House netted 18 arrests and $20,000 worth of gambling equipment. Owner Jimmy Brink was called to the U.S. Senate to possibly testify on Northern Kentucky's role in the nation's illegal gaming. The Lookout House closed and remained closed for a decade.

Fort Wright became a fifth-class city by decree of the 1954 Kentucky Legislature. The first mayor was Irving Widmyer and the council members were Werner Berkemeyer, Henry Nienaber, Leo Feltel, George Huser, and Charles Robke. Clifford Sander was council clerk and George Huser was city treasurer. In 1955, Fort Wright officials were congratulating the firefighters for attaining the position as one of the best volunteer fire departments in the state. "This attainment is no mere boost, but is evidenced by the low insurance rates which we enjoy as citizens and the respect given us by many officials of the state and their organizations in transacting business," wrote Mayor Widmyer in the July 1955 city newsletter.

As the decade ended and a new one began, new histories were made. In July 1958, Fort Wright residents were met with new sights every day as the interstate was constructed through Fort Wright and Fort Mitchell. During the building of the interstate, the 1840 Kyles homestead would be used as an equipment shed, and then it was razed. In 1962, Bill Finke and his brother opened Finke's Meat Market in Lookout Heights. The business would become a Northern Kentucky landmark. Likewise, Bill Melton bought Walt's Hitching Post on Madison Pike, a business that thrives today and harkens back to the BBQ stands of the 1920s tourist heyday. On the other end of Madison, though, Holy Guardian Angel Church was merged to Edgewood. Sandfordtown had formed a fire department on Madison Pike in around 1950, and after being renamed Southern Hills, it too ultimately merged with Edgewood.

From 1959 to 1978, Kentucky closed the public kindergarten system. Responding to public need, Betty White operated a private kindergarten from her Fort Wright home. Another operated in the city's St. Paul's Church. The South Hills Civic Club opened in 1957, and that city merged with Fort Wright in 1960. Lakeview, covering most of Madison Pike, was incorporated the same year. Bluegrass Swim Club opened in 1961, and the Lookout House reopened in 1962. In 1963, Nick Kreutzjans, George's brother, continued residential development in Lookout Heights, and Ben Wessels began work on the Sleepy Hollow apartments and other projects. In 1965, George Kreutzjans Sr. deeded more than 16 acres to the city, which would become the Nature Center.

In 1963, the Lookout Heights Municipal Building was built under Mayor Al Beasley. The Lookout Heights Civic Club was built in 1964. In 1968, Fort Wright and Lookout Heights merged. Fort Wright began to earn its nickname as the "City of Cities." "Fort Wright has that something special," *Kentucky Post* columnist Jim Reis wrote in 1985, when he examined "the city they all seem to want." In 1977, Fort Wright and Lakeview merged. And in 1980, a 20-year dispute between Fort Wright and Covington over annexed land ended with Fort Wright officially gaining the Fort Henry and General Drive areas.

As Fort Wright entered the 1980s, a plan to make Fort Wright a business hub started to take shape. The Lookout House had burned down in 1973 and was never rebuilt. In 1983, the Lookout Corporate Center was constructed on that former site as the city incentivized the transformation of the former Gourmet Strip into a business row. Ground was broken on the Fort Wright Municipal Building at Kyles Lane and Highland Pike in 1990. In 1995, Fort Wright was named "Northern

Kentucky's Most Livable City" by *Cincinnati Magazine*. The city came full circle in 2005, officially dedicating the James A. Ramage Civil War Museum, an entity dedicated to keeping alive the city's historical roots. This book seeks to establish a photographic record of the city's rich history.

Having now passed its golden 50th anniversary, Fort Wright has more than 5,600 people (2000 census) and about 250 businesses. Fort Wright is the headquarters location of several pillars of the region's services, the Kenton County Board of Education, the Transit Authority of Northern Kentucky (TANK), and Sanitation District One (SD1). At the two ends of the city are the 50-year-old businesses that serve as iconic historic landmarks, Finke's Meats and Walt's Hitching Post. Since its earliest days, Fort Wright has leveraged the assets that nearly come with proximity to Cincinnati, yet Fort Wright never lost its neighbors-helping-neighbors camaraderie.

The city is replete with people and families who have lived here for generations. The late Otto Siegrist, who built more than 100 homes in the city, told the *Kentucky Enquirer* in 1998, "Fort Wright has just plain old common people, and they all help each other out." Barbara Hellmann has lived in 18 tristate homes, but she has retired in Fort Wright. She said, "I've tried other places, but I always keep coming back here. There's nobody in the world like these neighbors."

One

A READY DEFENSE

For 13 days in September 1862, Maj. Gen. Horatio Wright, commander of the department of Ohio, and Gen. Lew Wallace protected Cincinnati. Confederate general Henry Heth entered Kentucky with a plan to march on Covington. From there, the Confederates planned to take Cincinnati. General Heth slowed his advance by raiding farms along the way, sending spoils back south. This permitted greater time for Union military preparation, including rallying forces.

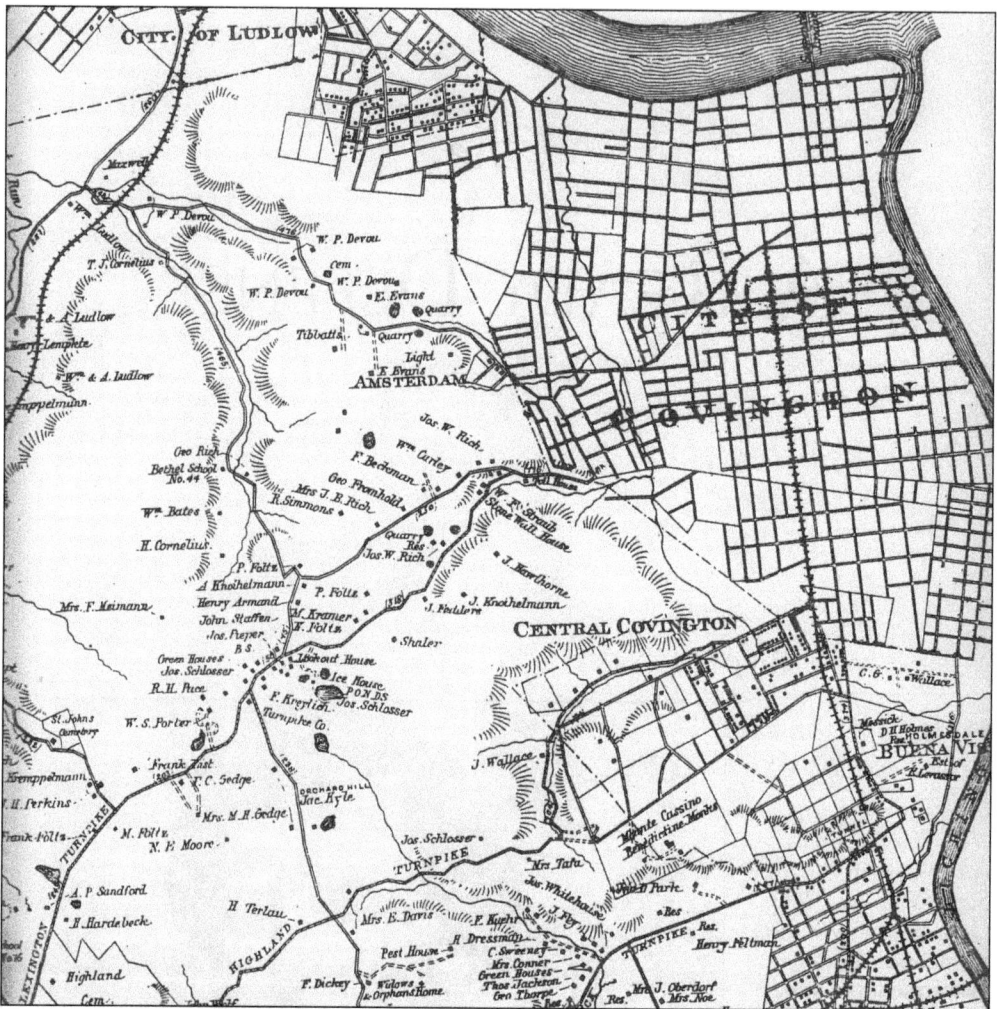

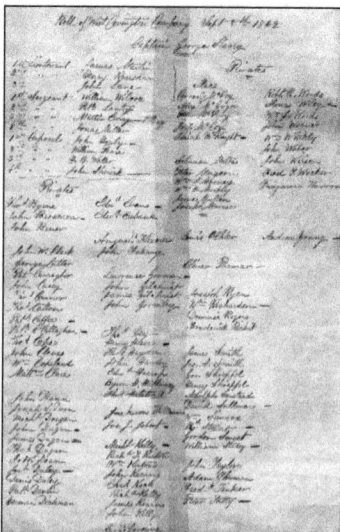

On September 3, 1862, the generals called laborers to build an 8-mile line of earthen defenses from Ludlow to Fort Thomas across the farm area that would become modern Fort Wright. Thousands of neighbors volunteered, including 1st Lt. James Martin. Martin, whose original signature is on this 1862 roll, is the great-grandfather of Don Martin Sr., Fort Wright mayor from 1989 to 1993. The defenses were built in three days. Strategic points were later expanded to include batteries and forts. "In a remarkably brief span of time our city, which was almost wholly defenseless, was in a state that would have enabled it to defy the whole rebel force in Kentucky with complete success. Strong works were erected—arose apparently in a night—and behind them were well placed thousands of riflemen," read a Cincinnati editorial.

Fort Wright sits less than 5 miles south of Cincinnati across the Ohio River, as pictured here. By September 9, 1862, a flotilla of steamboats holding 2,000 troops patrolled the river. The Northern Kentucky earthen fortifications and river patrol led General Heth and the Confederate army to abandon plans for the attack and withdraw. On September 15, 1862, a *Cincinnati Daily Enquirer* headline trumpeted, "The Rebel Movement on Cincinnati Frustrated."

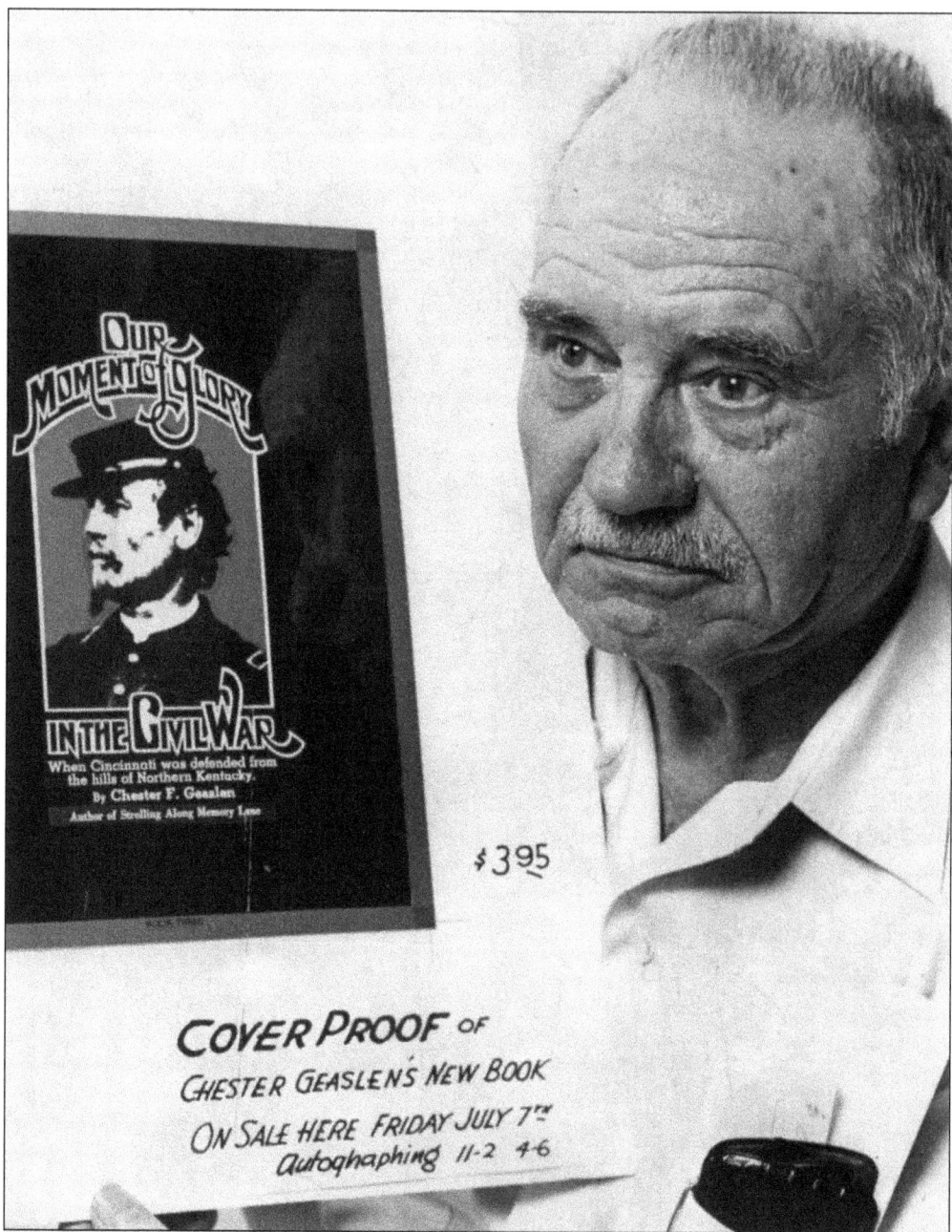

The earthen defenses are detailed by the late Chester Geaslen, a one-time Fort Wright resident, in *Our Moment of Glory*. Today's Kyle's Lane was the Robert Kyle farm (then Wolf Road) and later Kyle Battery. Nearby were Fort Wright (Horatio Wright's namesake), Fort Henry, McRae Battery (present-day Notre Dame Academy), Battery Hooper (on Highland Avenue), Carlisle Battery (present-day St. Charles Nursing Home), and Burbank Battery (overlooking Mother of God Cemetery).

14

FORT WRIGHT

Near here stood Fort Wright, built in Sept. 1862 by Union troops to help defend Cincinnati area from advancing Confederate armies. Fort named for Maj. Gen. Horatio G. Wright, USA, who later was chief engineer for completion of the Washington Monument. The city of Fort Wright is named for both the fort and the engineer-general.

Presented by Citizens of Fort Wright

The site of Civil War Fort Wright requires imagination. At that time, Highland Pike followed a creek from Banklick Turnpike (3-L) to the Lexington Turnpike (Dixie Highway). Around 1928, Highland Pike was reconstructed from Sandfordtown (3-L) along the hill directly across Kyle's Lane, connecting at Nineteenth Street to Covington. To accomplish this, the sites of Fort Wright and Kyle's Lane were cut down. The fort stood above today's historical marker No. 1917, where the two modern roads cross.

Of the 31 original Northern Kentucky batteries, Battery Hooper is one of only six remaining. Fern and Sheldon Storer preserved the site, covering it with dirt for the lawn of their Fort Wright home. Fern Storer was a well-known food editor for the *Cincinnati Post*. She died in 2002, and left her home and 14.5 acres to Northern Kentucky University (NKU). The city bought the property for $790,000 in 2004.

Dedicated in August 2005, the James A. Ramage Civil War Museum sits in a 17-acre city park. Named for an NKU history professor and Civil War author, the museum is on the first floor of the Storer home. The battery is being excavated by the city. Museum volunteers, like Kathleen Romero (left) and Mary DeSalvo, interpret history through reenactments at special events.

When troops threatened Cincinnati, as noted earlier, the *Cincinnati Enquirer* was briefly banned in Northern Kentucky, starting September 1, 1862. The *Covington Journal* suspended operations in protest of military censorship. Small businesses with no military importance were also suspended. When the threat abated, commerce resumed. Here in 1900, Joseph Jr. sits in a Fort Mitchell meat wagon at the Joseph Kuchle Horse Shoeing Wagon and Plow Workshop on Lexington Turnpike (Dixie Highway).

Early settlers travelled on trails created prehistorically by buffalo migration. In 1834, Kentucky chartered the Covington and Lexington Turnpike Road Company to build artificial roads. Around 1850, this macadamized portion of the Lexington Turnpike (Dixie Highway), running from Covington to Lexington, was being completed. This tollgate near Kyle's Lane shows Robert and Ellen Willis stopping a milkman. Milkmen were regular customers, and the toll saw farm goods pass that were going to Covington and Cincinnati. Responding to residents weary of tolls, the Kenton County Fiscal Court went to court in 1912 and gained control of the Lexington Turnpike within the county. This July 22, 1913, advertisement from the *Kentucky Post* indicates the sale of the Kyles Lane tollgate as road travel became toll-free. In 1916, the county was surfacing Dixie Highway with concrete at an approximate cost of $25,000 per mile.

FOR SALE.
TOLLHOUSES ON COVINGTON AND LEX-
INGTON TURNPIKE.

By order of the Kenton-co. Fiscal Court the tollhouses on the Covington and Lexington Turnpike will be sold at the Courthouse door, in Covington, Ky., July 30, at 10 o'clock a. m.

In early 1900, Joseph Moosbrugger's bakery truck sits in front Kuchle's blacksmith shop. On the goat cart are, from left to right, Alice, Helen, Ursala, Bertha, Josepha, Joseph Jr., and Carl Kuchle. The Kuchle home is in the background at the corner of Dixie Highway and Kyles Lane near the city's Pocket Park. The home is slated to be razed in the fall of 2009. A Walgreen's will be built.

A January 2, 1917, *Kentucky Post* headline announced, "Goldfish Farms Give Kenton County Nationwide Fame." The Schlosser Fisherman's Exchange on the Lexington Turnpike near Kyle's Lane was a national center for the profitable goldfish breeding industry. Joseph Schlosser pioneered the industry in the area. Other Fort Wright area dealers included Henry Knochelman of Highland Pike, J. Decker of the Lexington Turnpike, and Charles Speil of Amsterdam Pike.

This 1914 depiction of the Henry and Gus Knochelman farm shows a fence post along the drive and a pond dam that is now Henry Clay Avenue. Kyles Lane runs in front of the house and the barn, shown in the rear. The rail fence from Kyles Lane is now St. Anthony Circle. Part of this farm would later be sold to George Kreutzjans Sr. and Theodore Drees to build the city's first neighborhood.

Henry Knochelman
was featured in
a news story for
the development
of an irrigation
system. The barn
that had stood on
the farm for 125
years was razed
in March 1930.

This structure from the farm was Gus's Clubhouse, a place for the men on the farm to gather. It was located near modern-day Henry Clay Avenue.

Nine children were born to Mathias and Elizabeth Foltz, shown in 1908, at this 4-acre family farm. Located at approximately 1975 Dixie Highway, the house stood where Thriftway was later located. The farm had vegetables and chickens but no cattle. They earned a living selling vegetables to a Cincinnati commission (wholesale) house. Carl Lindner bought the house and 2 acres in 1961 for $70,000, and 2 acres were previously sold to a doctor.

Dr. Charles G. Pieck was a widely known Northern Kentucky physician and surgeon. His child Mildred is standing in the image, and his other children Edward and Louise are seated from left to right at his country residence at 1953 Pieck Drive in approximately 1905. On November 1, 1928, the Covington Park Board paid tribute to Dr. Pieck for his 22 years of board service as a founding board member and longtime vice president.

Two

ONE STREET AT A TIME

In 1930, George Kreutzjans Sr. left Lorup, Germany. That year he first saw the area that became Fort Wright. The "father of Fort Wright" built more than 200 homes in early Fort Wright, and he served more than 20 years on city council. He once said it went up "one street at a time." Pictured are, from left to right, sons Tony, John, Henry, George Sr., sons Nick, George Jr., and William, and George's wife, Barbara.

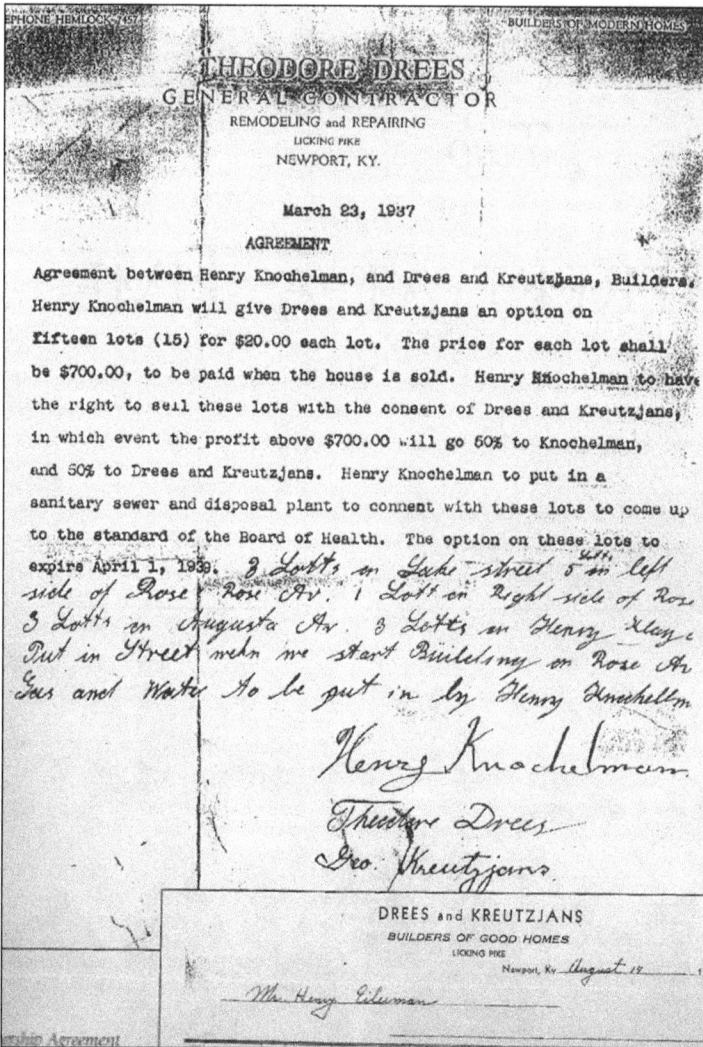

THEODORE DREES
GENERAL CONTRACTOR
REMODELING and REPAIRING
LICKING PIKE
NEWPORT, KY.

March 23, 1937

AGREEMENT

Agreement between Henry Knochelman, and Drees and Kreutzjans, Builders.
Henry Knochelman will give Drees and Kreutzjans an option on
fifteen lots (15) for $20.00 each lot. The price for each lot shall
be $700.00, to be paid when the house is sold. Henry Knochelman to have
the right to sell these lots with the consent of Drees and Kreutzjans,
in which event the profit above $700.00 will go 50% to Knochelman,
and 50% to Drees and Kreutzjans. Henry Knochelman to put in a
sanitary sewer and disposal plant to connect with these lots to come up
to the standard of the Board of Health. The option on these lots to
expire April 1, 1939. 3 Lotts on Lake street 5 on left
side of Rose Rose Av. 1 Lott on Right side of Rose
3 Lotts on Augusta Av. 3 Lotts on Henry Klage
Put in Street when we start Building on Rose Av
Gas and Water to be put in by Henry Knochellm

Henry Knochelman
Theodore Drees
Geo. Kreutzjans

DREES and KREUTZJANS
BUILDERS OF GOOD HOMES
LICKING PIKE
Newport, Ky August 18

Mr. Henry Eileman

By 1937, farmer Henry Knochelman became a developer. He entered an agreement with Theodore Drees and Kreutzjans, a Drees employee. Houses were often built one at a time since sales were challenging, but they constructed about seven homes in a row. The area lacked public transportation, which complicated the sale. Few could afford both car and house payments. Once the first home on Lake Street and Kennedy Road sold, the rest went within 10 days.

The one-and-a-half-story Cape Cods stood side by side on 40-foot-by-59-foot-wide and 100-foot-deep lots. The upstairs was often unfinished, so families could add on as they grew. Decorative mantelpieces with no functional purpose often adorned the living room. A brick arch graces many front porches. A coal-fired furnace heated the rooms.

On the pony are, from left to right, Lorraine Tink, Martha Rehkamp, and George Jr. Rehkamp in 1933. On January 9, 1940, the *Kentucky Post* reported that George Rehkamp joined Drees, Kreutzjans, and Fred Staengle to defray the cost of expanding bus service to South Hills and Fort Wright. Upon completion of the Knochelman lots, Drees and Kreutzjans bought undeveloped land from Rehkamp, a dairy farmer, to continue building.

An advertisement for the 1927 opening of the Heart's Desire subdivision of South Hills is pictured here. Realtor Fred Staengle was selling 448 lots at Highland Pike and Kyles Lane featuring $250,000 in city improvements. The pictured one-floor model bungalow had a gabled patio, pine trim, stone chimney, and stucco-walled living room.

Carl and Annetta Bishop built their first home in 1940 at 7 Glazier Road in Fort Wright. Pictured here in 1950, they raised their children Carl, Tom, Ben, Sally (Arlinghaus), Mary (Herzog), Katie (Wolnitzek), and Ted. Carl worked for the Union Light, Heat and Power Company for 48 years. Annetta was a homemaker, volunteer, and an active member in the Barrington Woods Homemakers Club.

In 1950, developers removed a home from Augusta Avenue that an 1820 deed called the "old homestead." Under the white clapboard shingles were the original hand-hewn timbers and log cabin that stood on a 100-acre parcel known as Kennedy Place. Kreutzjans bought the parcel for residential development.

This is Lorup Avenue being developed in the 1950s. The right center shows the duplex home alongside Ann Court. Lorup Avenue is named for Lorup, Germany, birthplace of several early Fort Wright residents.

In 1937, master builder Nikolaus Kreutzjans, George Sr.'s younger brother, expressed interest in leaving Lorup, Germany, for Fort Wright. World War II put his plans on hold. In 1948, Nikolaus applied for his papers. Days before Christmas in 1951, Lorup neighbors gathered to bid farewell to Nikolaus and Marie Kreutzjans, their daughter Anna, and infant son Rudy. Several builders would leave Lorup for Fort Wright and gain prominence in Northern Kentucky.

The Nikolaus Kreutzjans family lived with George's family at 13 Augusta Avenue on their arrival. George was building a Barbara Circle home for Mr. and Mrs. Bob Meyers. However, the Meyers agreed to occupy the next house built so Nikolaus's family could move into their own home at 2 Barbara Circle. Nikolaus and Marie Kreutzjans boarded a number of Lorup immigrants in their home, including John Fincken, Matth Toebben, Agnes Toebben Wessels, William Gerdes, and others.

Nick Kreutzjans went on to build about 200 homes between the Hazelwood and Fort Henry subdivisions in the Lookout Heights area. He is pictured in the 1963 Cavalcade of Homes with show organizers.

Also from Lorup, Germany, Ben Wessels moved to Fort Wright in 1960. Pictured here in 1963 with his land surveyors transit, he starts construction of the Devou Village Apartments. He also constructed homes on Vidot Court and Park Road, apartments on Diamond Court and Sleepy Hollow near St. Agnes, and office buildings on Dixie Highway. He met his wife, Agnes Toebben, also from Lorup, once he was in the United States.

Shown here are Bernie and Carlo Wessels, Ben's sons, at a Sleepy Hollow job site. Bernie, Rick, and Carlo are associated with the family business today. They built Wrights Summit on Dixie Highway. Bernie Wessels has also served on Fort Wright City Council, as a board member of the city business association, and as a representative to both the Kenton County Planning Commission and the Northern Kentucky Area Planning Commission.

This is Fort Henry Drive being poured in approximately 1965. The Fort Henry and General Drive areas would become the source of a 20-year annexation dispute between Covington and Fort Wright.

In early Fort Wright, many gatherings took place in the basements of homes, including planning meetings for the Fort Wright Civic Club, meetings for the development of the fire department, some council meetings, and an occasional party.

From left to right, Nick Toebben of Germany, Nick and Maria Kreutzjans, Judy and John Toebben, Ben and Agnes Wessels, and Laverne and Matth Toebben eat at the Fort Wright Lookout House around 1970.

Tom Terlau, 18 years old (left), and Bill Vocke work on a Fort Wright home.

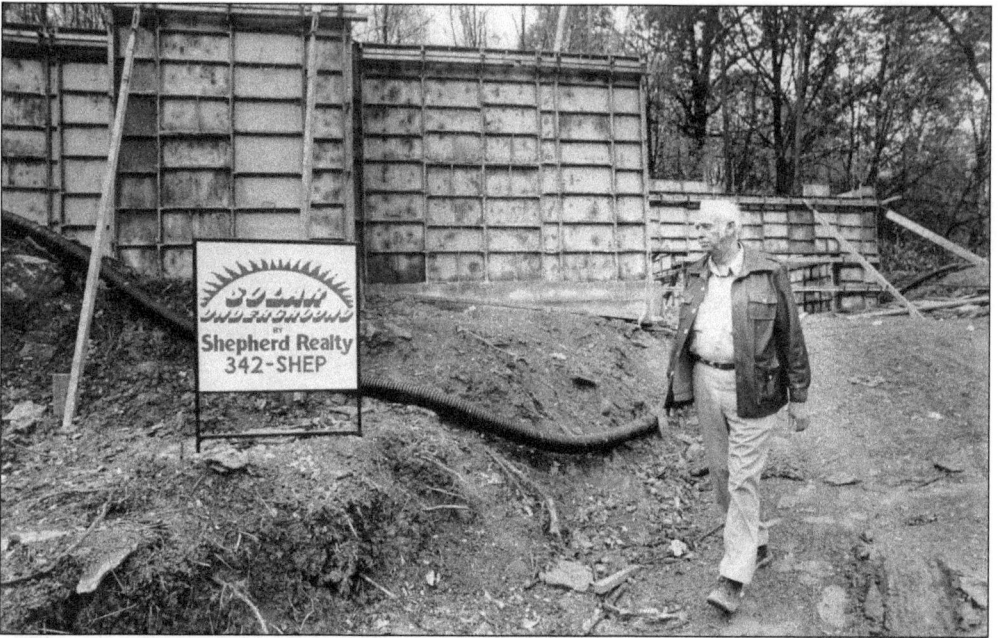

Harold Shepherd, 60 years old, inspects a Fort Wright home he is building on November 7, 1977. The breakthrough underground house on Henry Clay Avenue was a solar home.

The ribbon is cut on a Homefest event at Beaumont Court featuring Fort Wright mayor John McCormack and vice mayor Joe Nienaber, Chuck Berling, Rudy Kreutzjans, and officials from the home-builders association.

Homefest, a showcase of new Fort Wright homes and innovations, continues.

This photograph showcases the day's state-of-the-art street signs at St. Anthony and Marcella Streets. The city installed the modern street signs, which featured reflective properties.

The state opened bids for the initial building of Interstate 75 (I-75) in June 1958. The first stretch was built from Covington, through Fort Wright to Fort Mitchell. The front page of the July 15, 1958, *Kentucky Post* said Dixie Highway motorists saw new sites daily as building progressed. This September 25, 1968, photograph of I-75 North shows the Kyles Lane and Lookout Heights exit at the Fort Wright line.

The building of the interstate lent a *Wizard of Oz* chapter to Fort Wright's history. George Scheper built the home at 5 Highview Street, and in 1958, his home got a new neighbor in an unusual way. The home across the street from his was uprooted, as shown here, and moved intact to 3 Highview Street to make way for the building of the interstate.

Three

THE LEXINGTON TURNPIKE

The Lexington Turnpike became Dixie Highway, a major area thoroughfare. This 1952 aerial photograph shows the Lookout House, center, and the Stephens goldfish farm in the upper left. St. Agnes Church is in the upper right. The frame structure behind the church is the school, built in 1941. The rectory and annex are absent, as they would be added later. This area was Lookout Heights at the time.

In 1886, Alois Hampel bought Rush's Tavern, tore it down, and built a three-story building topped at the corner with a cupola. Patrons could climb the stairs "to the highest point in Northern Kentucky," and the Lookout House was born. In 1912, Bill Hill bought the Lookout, and the fame of the diner grew. In 1933, Jimmy Brink became operator and renovated the Lookout to a plush club and gaming spot.

The Lookout House becomes a showplace of the nation. A 1951 state raid of the Lookout House netted 18 arrests and $20,000 worth of gambling equipment. The club was closed, but it would reopen in 1961 without the casino.

As shown on Bernie Spencer's Northern Kentucky Views Web site, in March 1951, the *Times Star* reported that Jimmy Brink (left) was called to report to the office of U.S. Senate sergeant-at-arms Joseph Duke (right) to be a possible congressional Kefauver Commission witness. The U.S. Senate spokesperson indicated that Brink might be asked about gambling in Northern Kentucky. Brink died in an airplane crash in 1952.

In this era, the Lookout House anchored Northern Kentucky's Gourmet Strip, which dominated Dixie Highway, winding through Park Hills and Fort Wright. Jack's Tavern, pictured here, is approximately where Skyline's is today. A 1983 *Kentucky Post* column indicated that the Gourmet Strip outshone Cincinnati with food and gambling. Fine restaurants included the White Horse and Town and Country.

Oelsner's Colonial Inn was part of the Gourmet Strip. Owner Russell Oelsner was the mayor of Lookout Heights for 14 years and was a Kenton County deputy sheriff. Lookout Heights would merge with Fort Wright in 1968. Oelsner sold the inn, restaurant, and tavern in 1960. The tavern was popular with members of the Cincinnati Reds and the St. Agnes Chapter of the Catholic War Veterans, according to Jim Reis of the *Kentucky Post*.

One of Main Dining Rooms

Mason Dixon Cocktail Lounge

Oelsner's Colonial Tavern

This vintage postcard of Oelsner's showcases the main dining room and cocktail lounge. Oelsner's was popular in the 1930s and sat opposite the Lookout House.

DANA ANDREWS
CANYON PASSAGE
SUSAN HAYWARD
WAHOO SCREEN GAME FRIDAY

BURGER

One of Northern Kentucky's first drive-ins, the Dixie Gardens, opened on the Gourmet Strip in what was then Lookout Heights on July 3, 1947. The approximately 25 acres of property showed movies for more than two decades, and the property at one time also held an ice-skating rink. The *Times Star* said thousands attended a 1957 Easter egg hunt at the Dixie Gardens.

Meanwhile, Joseph Kuchle saw his Dixie Highway blacksmith business morph into a car garage. Only blacksmiths could straighten Ford's Model T shafts. In 1919, rock was quarried from the hill below St. Charles to Kyles Lane to build the foundation of the Kuchle car garage, which was finished in January 1922. In 1946, the Kuchle sons added a showroom to market new cars, according to published Kuchle family histories.

The Kuchle Garage sold Crosleys, Lincoln Mercurys, and Kaisers for a time. Around 1973, the business passed to grandsons, who determined there was enough business to open two garages, according to published Kuchle family histories. The Fort Wright location was renamed the Roger Kuchle Garage, while the Fort Mitchell Garage was opened 2 miles north on Dixie Highway in Park Hills.

Carl Kuchle, the oldest of the 13 children of Joseph Kuchle, stands next to the new wrecker. In the early 1900s, a man named John Decker ran a wagon shop, greenhouse, and florist across from Kuchle's. At the time, Decker's Lane, now Tower Hill Shopping Center area, was the namesake of John Decker.

A streetcar line started in Fort Mitchell, came down Dixie Highway through Fort Wright behind Decker's Lane, and through Park Hills to Covington. This March 28, 1948, Easter Day photograph shows Bev and Phyllis Hayden catching the trolley to the movies. Residents say the fare was a nickel, except a school pass was 2.5¢.

Schilling's Motel and Restaurant
U.S. 25 AND 42, COVINGTON, KY.
2½ MILES SOUTH OF CINCINNATI

This postcard of Schilling's Motel and Restaurant promotes the Dixie Highway, Fort Wright establishment. The 1957 fire featured on this book's cover occurred at Schilling's Restaurant, on the far right of the postcard.

- Fireproof
- Central Heating
- Individual Air Conditioning
- 24 Hour Service
- Comfortably and Tastefully Furnished
- Ample Parking Space
- Conference Room
- FREE TV — Each Room
- Direct Dial Service
- Swimming Pool
- 225 Rooms

LAMPLIGHTER MOTOR INN
AND Hofbrau Haus RESTAURANT
1939 DIXIE HIGHWAY   COVINGTON, KENTUCKY
PHONE 331-1400 AREA CODE 606

This postcard for the Lamplighter Motor Inn and Hofbrau Haus on Dixie Highway in Fort Wright promotes 225 sleeping rooms, a swimming pool, and individual air-conditioning.

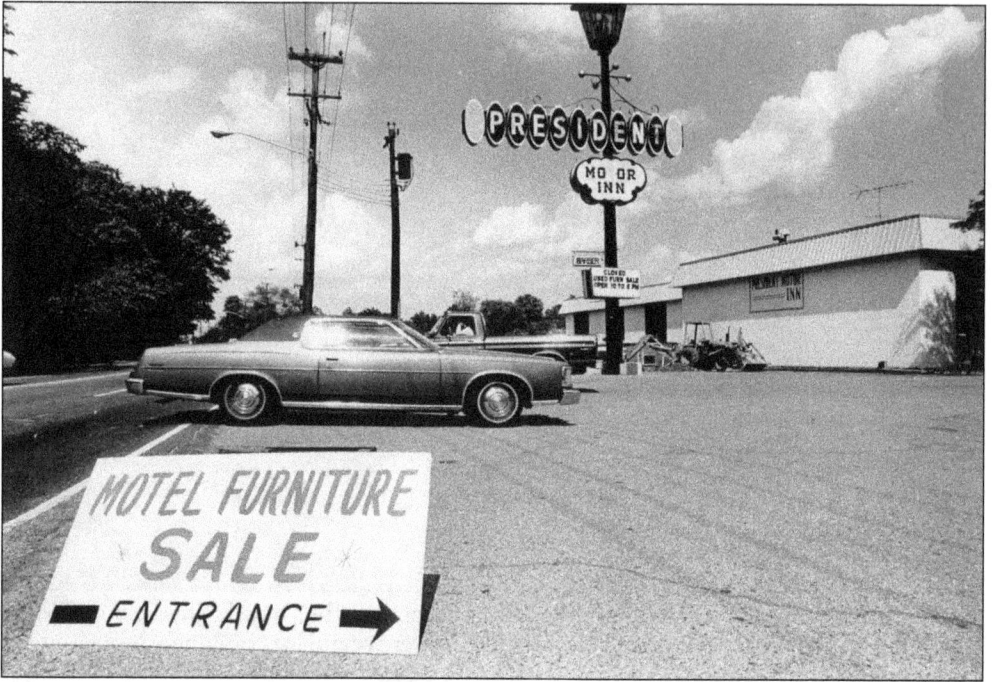

During an overnight stay around 1960, the Secret Service tightened guard on Republican presidential nominee Richard Nixon at Fort Wright's President's Motor Inn, pictured here in 1978. Fire chief Pete Nienaber said flames in a vacant old Foltz property house about 150 yards from the hotel were quickly extinguished. Nienaber stated the fire appeared to be intentionally set, and charred Nixon posters were in the cabinet of origin. No one was injured.

Let it be known that we of the fabulous Lookout House hereby welcome and invite the Beatles... Ringo, Paul, John, George, their managers and associates to hold the press conference of August 20th at our establishment, 1721 Old Dixie Highway, Covington, Kentucky.

The Casino Room is at your disposal, accommodating up to 1,000 attendees, and private dressing rooms for your convenience.

It has been our pleasure in the past to host many famous American entertainers. We have never, however, had a group from England. The Lookout House will make any arrangements necessary to satisfy your needs. Our establishment reflects the culture of your group and we'd love being your host.

Richard J. Schilling
owner of the Lookout House

After sitting idle for 10 years, the Lookout was bought by brothers Robert and Richard Schilling in 1962, and they reestablished the elaborate dining place, which saw entertainers like Frank Sinatra, the Four Seasons, and Jimmy Durante. In this photograph, Richard Schilling tried to lure the Beatles to the Lookout, making the large main casino room available to them. A lunch menu shows a 95¢ hamburger and a skillet-fried half chicken for $2.95.

On August 14, 1973, a $2 million fire leveled the Lookout House. It was the largest fire the city's fire department had yet responded to. The fire chief and most department officers were more than five hours away, attending the state fire convention. Lt. Bob Becker led the efforts of a half-dozen fire departments, 140 men, and 13 vehicles.

Firemen said the intense heat kept them from getting to the fire at first. It spread rapidly because the building was divided into many irregularly shaped rooms and had many false ceilings, as remodeling had been underway.

A crowd of approximately 1,000 people gathered to watch the blaze that gutted the entire interior of the establishment.

Working on the fire are, from left to right, Jeff Lee, Ron Becker, and Tom Droege.

46

Fort Mitchell fireman William Kennedy is loaded onto a stretcher as, from left to right, Paul Schewe, reporter Mike Kennedy, and Bob Becker look on. Kennedy was on an aerial ladder and caught his foot between two rungs. He had to slip out of his boot to free himself. He was treated and released at the hospital, and no other injuries were sustained. The Lookout House was never rebuilt.

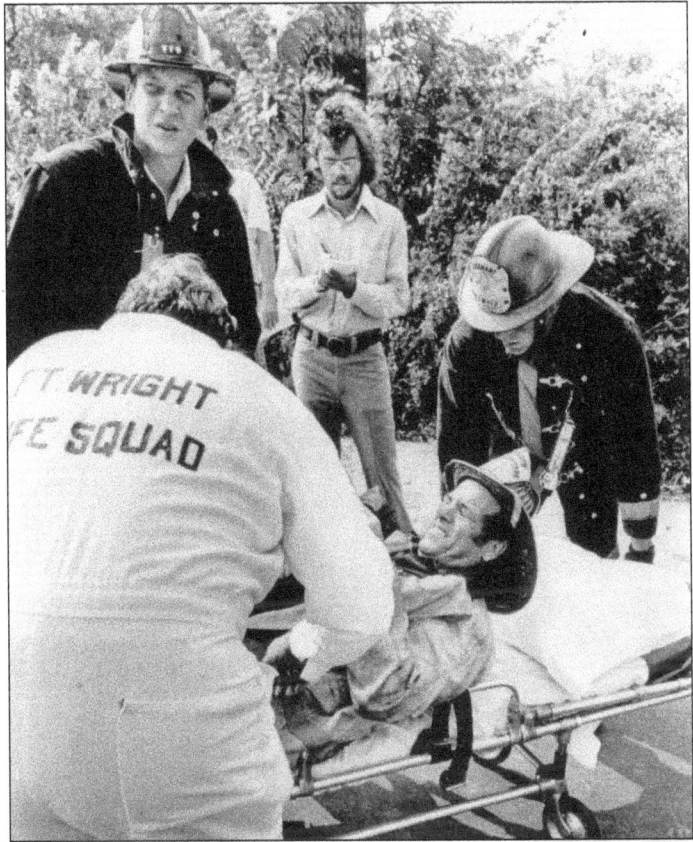

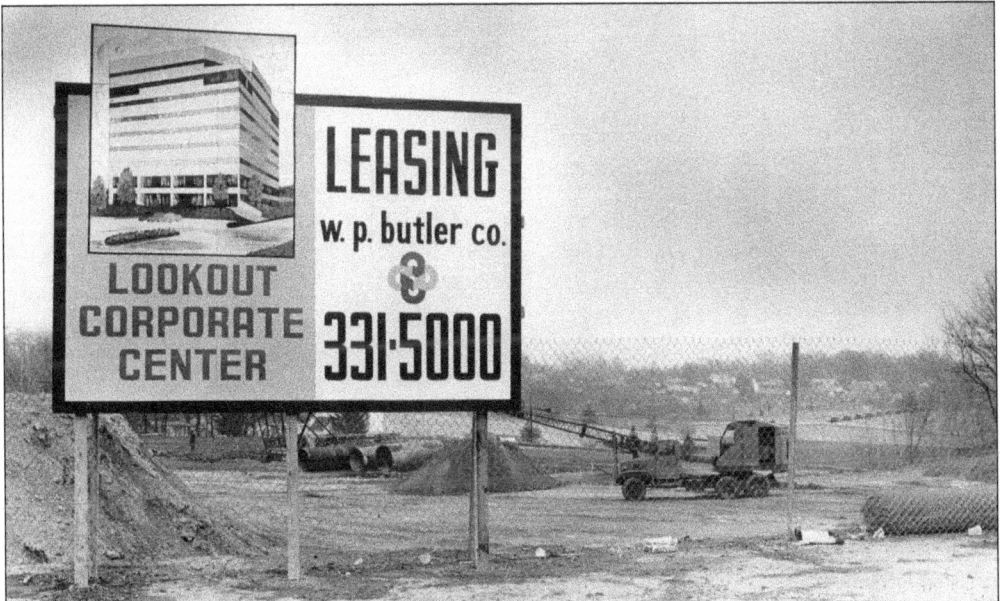

A decade after the fire, city fathers began a plan to transform the Gourmet Strip into a Northern Kentucky business hub. The Lookout Corporate Center was built on the site of the former Lookout House, starting in 1983. The hill upon which the Lookout stood was leveled.

This nine-story building was among the largest suburban Cincinnati office complexes at the time, and it became a catalyst for other redevelopment. Citizens National Bank built next door. The bank president told newspapers the site was picked for its "great location. It's very visible [on I-75] and near to both Cincinnati and the Fort Wright-Fort Mitchell area."

Construction for Fort Wright Executive Centers I and II began at the same time at the Fort Wright corner of Dixie Highway and Rivard Drive. Developer Ben Wessels told the newspaper that the site was selected for the main highway (Dixie), good exposure, low taxes, and availability of bonds, and "we will complement the Butler building (Lookout Center)." The Fort Wright business row was born.

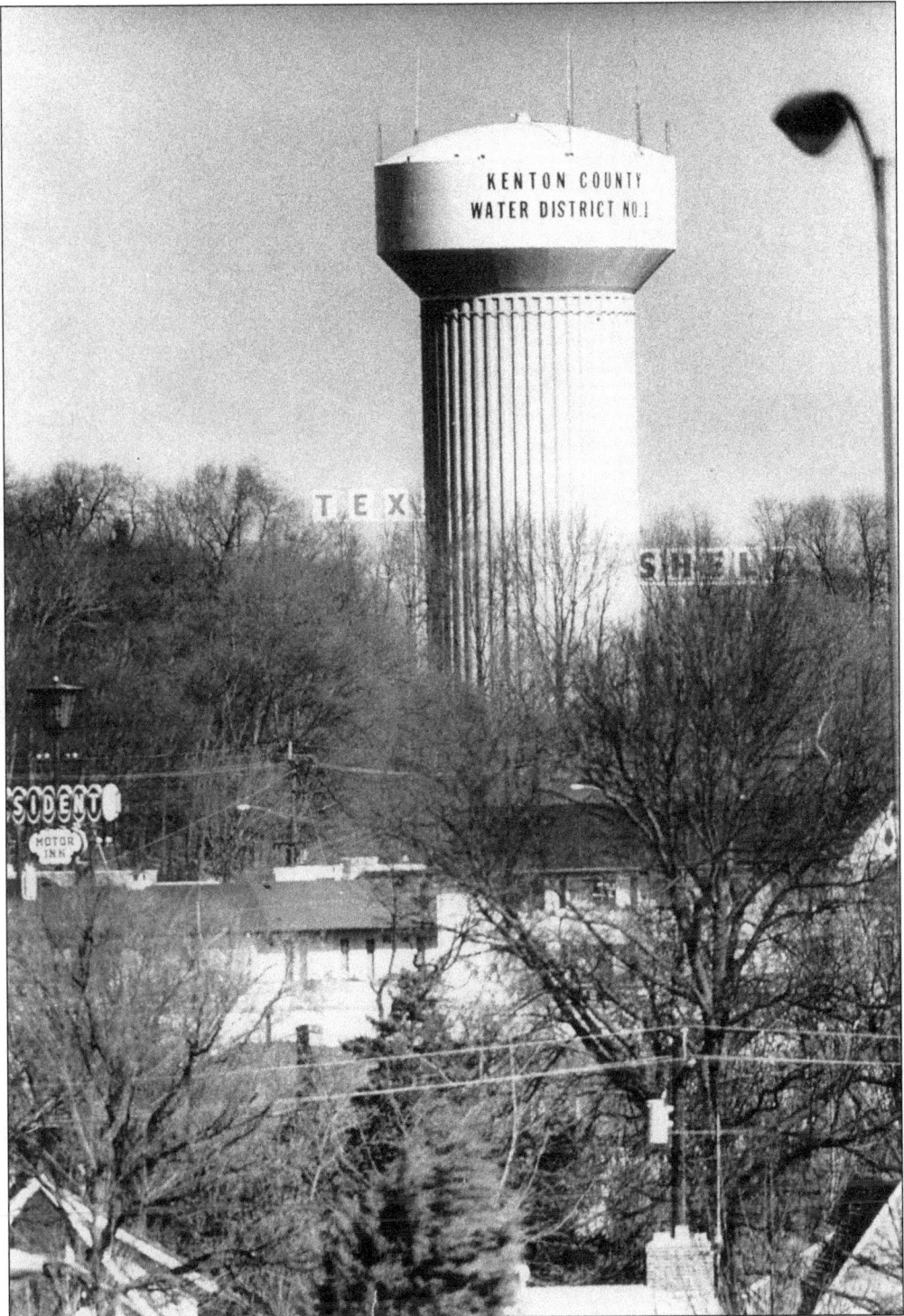

The Kenton County Water District tower has been in Fort Wright for many decades. At one time, it was a smaller tank on lattice legs. Around the 1960s, the current one-million-gallon tank was built.

Just miles from Cincinnati at the top left, a mid-1980s aerial view of Fort Wright's Dixie Highway would look like this. Kyles Lane over Interstate 75, pictured in the lower right, provided high visibility and convenient access for developers. The Lookout Corporate Center, near the center, would catalyze business development along Dixie Highway. The Dixie Gardens drive-in, near the center of the picture to the left of the interstate, would close, awaiting development.

Four

THE BANKLICK TURNPIKE

The area that became Fort Wright contained two turnpikes from Cincinnati to Lexington, the Lexington Turnpike (Dixie Highway) and the Banklick Turnpike (Madison Pike or 3-L Highway). Over four years, Kenton County purchased 35 miles of turnpike, ending tolls in 1913. The 10-mile Banklick Turnpike between Latonia and Independence was bought for $16,000. This is the Henry Hahn Saloon and Four Mile House at Madison Pike and Eaton Drive around 1920.

In 1928, the Lexington and Banklick Turnpikes to Lexington ran parallel for about 100 miles. The Lexington Turnpike ran through Walton, Williamstown, and Georgetown, while Banklick ran through Independence, Falmouth, Cynthiana, and Paris. Dixie Highway was under construction four years, opening in 1928. During that time, all through traffic used Madison Pike, a huge business boon to service stations like this one, pictured in 1925 across from today's Walt's Hitching Post.

Eddy's Fischer Gas Station, pictured here in around 1930 at Madison Pike and Orphanage Road, was another beneficiary of having Madison Pike as the primary route. The *Kentucky Post* reported as many as 1,000 cars per day passed through at the height of tourist season. The Highway Commission moved the designation U.S. 25 to Dixie Highway when it opened in November 1928, leaving Madison Pike with U.S. 27.

While entrepreneurs along the Madison Pike route had been building up services like garages, restaurants, and roadside fruit and barbecue stands for several years, as shown here, tourist business was reported to have dried up almost overnight when Dixie Highway opened. Newspapers noted that Madison Pike remained a nationally known, navigable, and scenic route. However, Dixie Highway had fewer curves and was a few miles shorter to Lexington.

The 1928 *Kentucky Post* opined, "The outcome of this unusual situation will be interesting. There undoubtedly is enough traffic to give both routes a share." This 1940s photograph shows the Farm Café at Madison Pike and Orphanage Road at the site of today's Bob Evans Restaurant.

Before electric refrigeration, ice was important in daily life. Brothers Joe and Phil Mueller owned Latonia Ice and Fuel Company. In the early 1900s, they harvested ice from the spring-fed Mueller Lake, one of several Madison Pike lakes. Latonia's ice kept produce in nearby railcars cold. The Transit Authority of Northern Kentucky (TANK) bus barn currently occupies the former lake area, and attorneys occupy Joe Mueller's adjacent stone house.

In 1864, settlers built a mission church and school in the area on the corner of today's Madison and Dudley Pikes. By 1885, a new church and school would be dedicated as Holy Guardian Angels Parish, according to the *History of the Diocese of Covington*. A new school was constructed in 1909, and this is a 1931 class photograph. The cemetery in the photograph remains at that corner today.

This is the altar of Holy Guardian Angel Parish around 1931. The parish numbered about 70 families by 1950. In 1955, concerned citizens met at the church to form Sandfordtown Fire Department, initially located on today's Madison Pike in Fort Wright. In 1958, the church and school closed when Edgewood's St. Pius X opened. Likewise, the Sandfordtown Fire Department eventually merged with the Edgewood Fire Department.

In around 1832, the 50-room, three-story Latonia Springs Hotel was built as a mineral water spa, according to Dr. Joseph Gastright. The springs thrived prior to the Civil War under operator Dr. Stephen Moser. However, the springs waned and an 1879 murder near the springs brought further attention to its disarray. This drawing is by Jim Kelly, as no known photograph exists. United Dairy Farmers now occupies the former hotel site.

Gastright wrote that just after 1891, August Ratermann and Herman Summe bought the land around the Latonia Springs Hotel for dairy farming. They used the spring to cool their product.

Operated by the Ratermann family, the Latonia Springs Picnic Grounds and Camp was operated in the area well through the 1930s, often hosting gypsy business and business from the Latonia Racetrack. The only building on the property was the one pictured. The camp was on a two-lane gravel road and campers typically pitched tents. The camp's popularity waned when the racetrack closed.

Bob Ratermann later ran an auto salvage yard for many years on the former hotel site. After his return from World War II, he began the business with parts and a wrecker stored in a family barn. He said he quickly earned wrecker business from surrounding police and communities on the pledge that he would provide around-the-clock service.

By 1950, Latonia Springs Auto Parts had more than 2,000 cars and a variety of salvage, with a booming wrecker business. The top of the picture shows Madison Pike. Highland Pike is pictured in the center left and shows through traffic, and Highland Pike leads to Dixie Highway. Ratermann served as treasurer of the Greater Cincinnati Salvage Association, and he had 17 employees when he retired from the business.

Ratermann recalls that he responded to as many as 13 auto wrecks in one weekend. He said people gathered at High's Sandwich Shop across from his lot or gawked on the drive by to see who wrecked their car. He said he once responded to the garage of his Dixie Highway competitor, the Kuchles. An auto ran into Kuchle Garage, causing significant damage. Their business awning collapsed and pinned in the Kuchle wrecker.

Ratermann also built the Latonia Springs Café building at Highland and Madison Pikes, later run by the Nageleisen family. Mr. Dickmann later assumed the café, pictured here. When Kentucky 17 was progressing, Dickmann's Café moved to a new location, where it is today off of Madison Pike on Orphanage Road.

The development in the upper right, formerly Latonia Springs Auto Parts, was occurring in around 2000 in preparation for today's Wal-Mart. The bottom center shows the administrative headquarters for Sanitation District One (SD1), the second-largest public sewer utility in Kentucky, overseeing nearly all Northern Kentucky systems. In 2004, SD1 built Public Service Park, an interactive environmental education opportunity for children. The Kenton County School District administrative headquarters are also pictured.

Around the year 2000, this view of Madison Pike shows, on the left side starting at the bottom, a driving range, a rental storage facility, an animal hospital, and the Transit Authority of Northern Kentucky (TANK) headquarters.

Moving from Newport, the Madison Pike TANK headquarters cornerstone was laid in Fort Wright in 1982. "This facility gives TANK a well-equipped maintenance shop, a bus storage area, a park and ride lot for passenger use, as well as close proximity to I-275 and I-75," says TANK's Web site. TANK provides bus service throughout Northern Kentucky and to downtown Cincinnati and carried 3.6 million passengers in 2004.

Around 1958, Bill Melton bought Walt's Hitching Post on Madison Pike, a historic barbecue joint harkening back to the road's boon years in the 1920s. Walt's still smokes their ribs outside, in a wood-fired pit, finishing them under the grill. Faulty wiring for neon lighting caused this 1995 fire. It was the first as a fire department officer for Steve Schewe, who became chief in 2001.

Five

CITY OF CITIES

Homes were built, buses ran, mail was on the way, and in 1941, Fort Wright incorporated as a city. Early officials are, from left to right, (first row) George Huser, Roy Willer, the first mayor Irving Widmyer, Bob Tranter, and Werner Berkmeyer; (second row) Urban Siegrist, unidentified, George Kreutzjans, John McCormack, Jack Conersman, Bob Meyer, and Otto Siegrist. Widmyer served as mayor from 1954 to 1961.

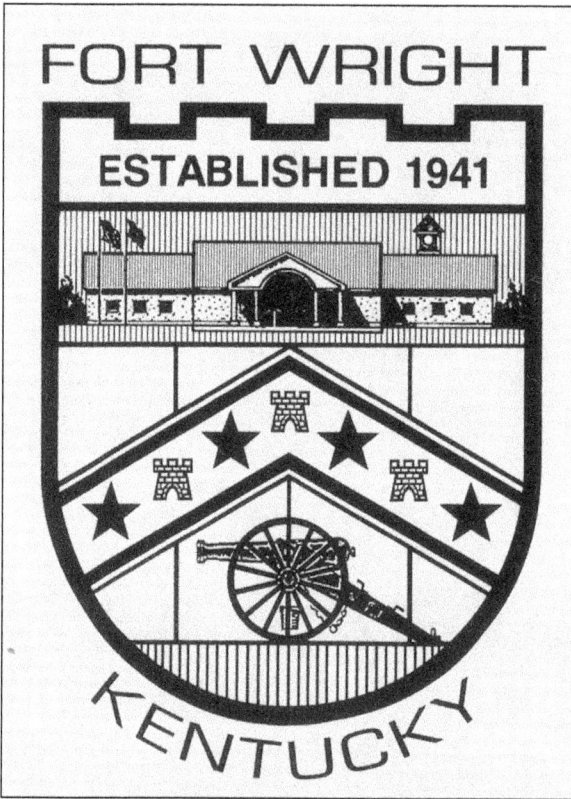

The Fort Wright motto is "City of Cities." Over time, Fort Wright grew, taking in the neighboring communities of South Hills, Lookout Heights, and Lakeview, as represented by the four stars on the city logo, according to some. "Fort Wright apparently has that something special," Jim Reis wrote in a *Kentucky Post* column titled, "The City They All Seem to Want." The Fort Wright Fire Department, developed in 1949, was an asset envied by neighbors.

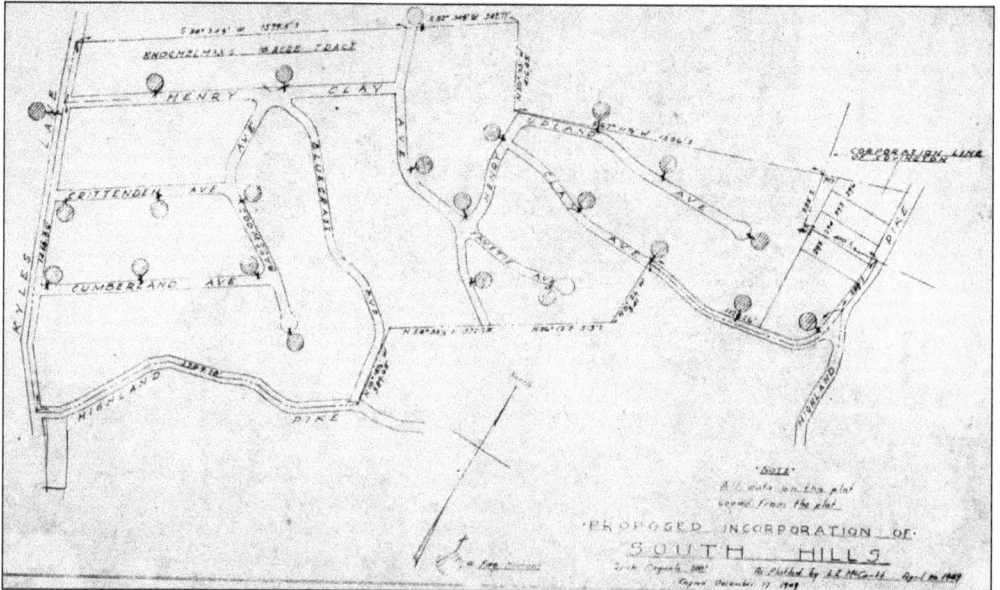

This is the 1949 incorporation map of South Hills. Its mayors were A. J. Rung, Royal Clark, George Schulte, and M. A. Groening. In 1960, the cities agreed to merge, and Fort Wright annexed South Hills. After drawing lots, Fort Wright councilmen John McCormack and George Huser stepped down from the council. South Hills trustees William Groening and Robert Saalfeld would replace them on the merged council. Huser was appointed treasurer.

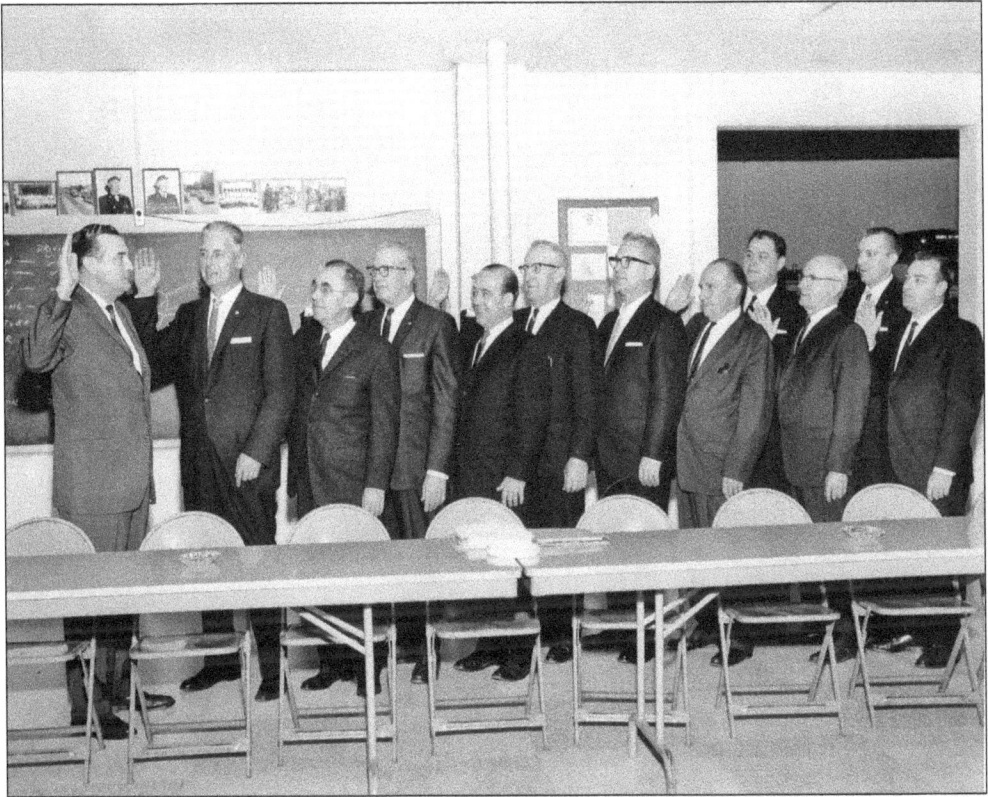

In the Fort Wright Firehouse, from left to right, Judge Goodenough swears in George Shepherd, an unidentified South Hills trustee, Fred Wolnitzek, Ralph Wisekettle, George Kreutzjans, Bud Tenhundfeld, former South Hills mayor George Schulte, Joe Summe, George Huser, Don Martin Sr., and Bob May.

Fred Wolnitzek served as mayor of Fort Wright from 1962 to 1977, making him the city's longest-serving mayor.

By 1962, Lookout Heights was bustling. The Lookout House reopened, Dixie Gardens thrived, and Bill Finke and his brother bought Yoder's and opened Finke's Meat Market at Sleepy Hollow and Amsterdam Roads. By 2003, Finke's was selling about 17,000 pounds of its signature goetta a year, using his great-grandfather's 1800s recipe. The *Business Courier* called Finke's a landmark for Northern Kentuckians.

Lookout Heights incorporated in 1937. Its mayors were Russell Oelsner, J. R. Blumlein, Howard Schambach, and Alfred Beasley. This 1963 municipal building ground-breaking features Beasley with the shovel. Fort Wright and Lookout Heights voters approved merger in 1967. Like with South Hills, the merger was viewed as providing better services and protection from Covington, which was targeting areas for annexation. Park Hills talked about a merger but dropped out.

The Lookout Heights Civic Club was built in 1964, and in 1968, it had an expansion that doubled its size. Having merged in 1968, the ribbon cutting that year featured, from left to right, Mayors Fred Wolnitzek and Alfred Beasley of Fort Wright-Lookout Heights. The civic club is still active, and for a time in history, served as Fort Wright City Hall.

This late-1960s photograph of Fort Wright officials shows, from left to right, (first row) Bill Snyder, George "Bud" Tenhunfeld, George Kreutzjans, Fred Wolnitzek, Dr. Dru, Bob Hebbler, and Bill with surname unknown; (second row) Otto Siegrist, Bob May, Joe Summe, Don Martin Sr., Bob Myers, George Huser, Virgle Moore, and John Elfers.

This 1974 photograph shows, from left right, (first row) council members Ray Schuler, Robert Lee, and George Schulte, Mayor Fred Wolnitzek, and council members Robert Hackman, William Mertes, and Thomas Wissel; (second row) city attorney Garry Edmondson, police clerk Virgil Moore, police judge Donald Martin Sr., police chief Robert Myers, county attorney John Elfers, Judge William Schaber, city clerk Dorothy Snyder, assistant clerk Mary Warken, and fire chief Pete Nienaber.

Fort Wright mayor Fred Wolnitzek presents Seal Huser with a proclamation naming George Huser Drive. In the back row are, from left to right, Bob Hackman, William Mertes, George Schulte, Bob Lee, Thomas Wissel, and Garry Edmondson.

Civic pride has always run long and marched proud in Fort Wright. Fourth of July parades had legions of bicycles, wagons, and walkers turn out to join the fire equipment and floats. This police car leads a parade on the West Crittenden Avenue block.

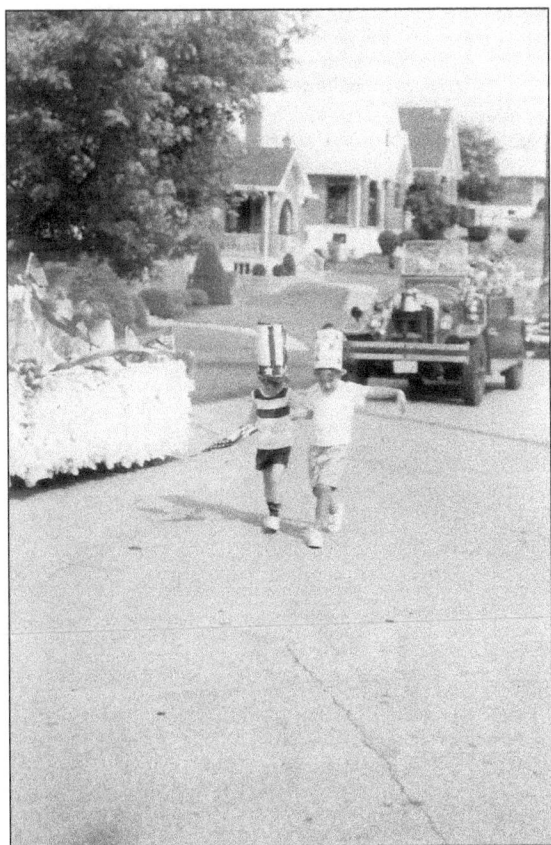

Todd Caton and Jim White are in the foreground of this 1971 Fourth of July parade.

The 1971 parade bicyclers come down West Henry Clay Avenue and reach the corner of Rosa Avenue. The bicycle battalion was a traditional part of every Fourth of July parade.

A photograph of Fort Wright City Council in 1976 shows, from left to right, (first row) William Snyder, Tom Litzler, Mayor Fred Wolnitzek, Norbert Cahill, and Thomas Widmyer; (second row) Elmer Muth, state representative Louis DeFlaide, and William Mertes.

Lakeview was the Madison Pike area named for its lakes, including the 10-acre lake where TANK now sits, goldfish ponds where Eaton Asphalt is, and Ratermann Lake that is now filled in. Running from Mother of God Cemetery to about Pioneer Park, it incorporated around 1960. Its mayors were McKinley Butcher, Nick Carlin, and Edward Rizzo. Both cities' voters approved merger in 1977.

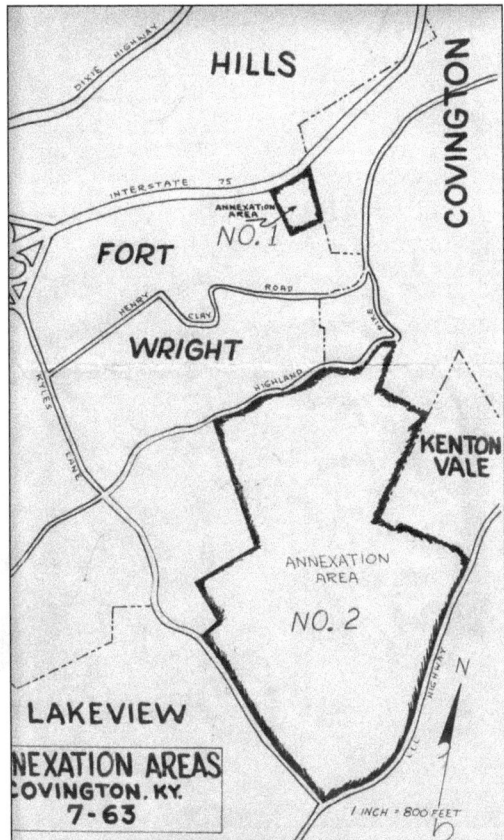

After the Lakeview merger, the size of the council was increased to eight for a time. This 1978 photograph shows, from left to right, Don Martin Sr.; city attorney Garry Edmondson; police chief Gene Weaver; former Lakeview mayor Edward Rizzo; Pat Dressman; Mayor Tom Litzler; council members Joe Nienaber, Dennis Halfhill, Al Witschy, and Tom Widmyer; city clerk Elmer Muth; and council member Norb Cahill.

This 1982 photograph shows, from left to right, council members Joe Nienaber and Betty Engelman, city attorney Edmondson, Mayor Tom Litzler, council member Frank Wolnitzek, Judge Judy West, and council members Frank Pohlgeers and Tom Jacober.

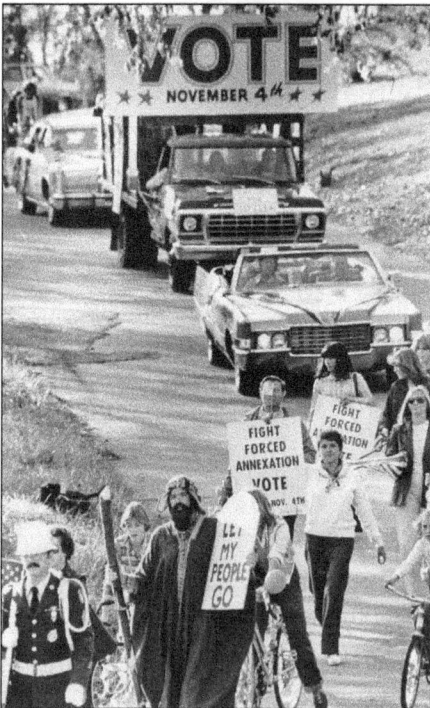

In 1983, Kenton Vale voted to merge with Fort Wright, but Fort Wright voters turned it down. The Fort Henry and General Drive area supported the merger, the only precinct that did. It might have been that way because this section of Fort Wright was the source of a court battle between Covington and Fort Wright for more than 20 years, ending in a vote and agreement that returned the area to Fort Wright.

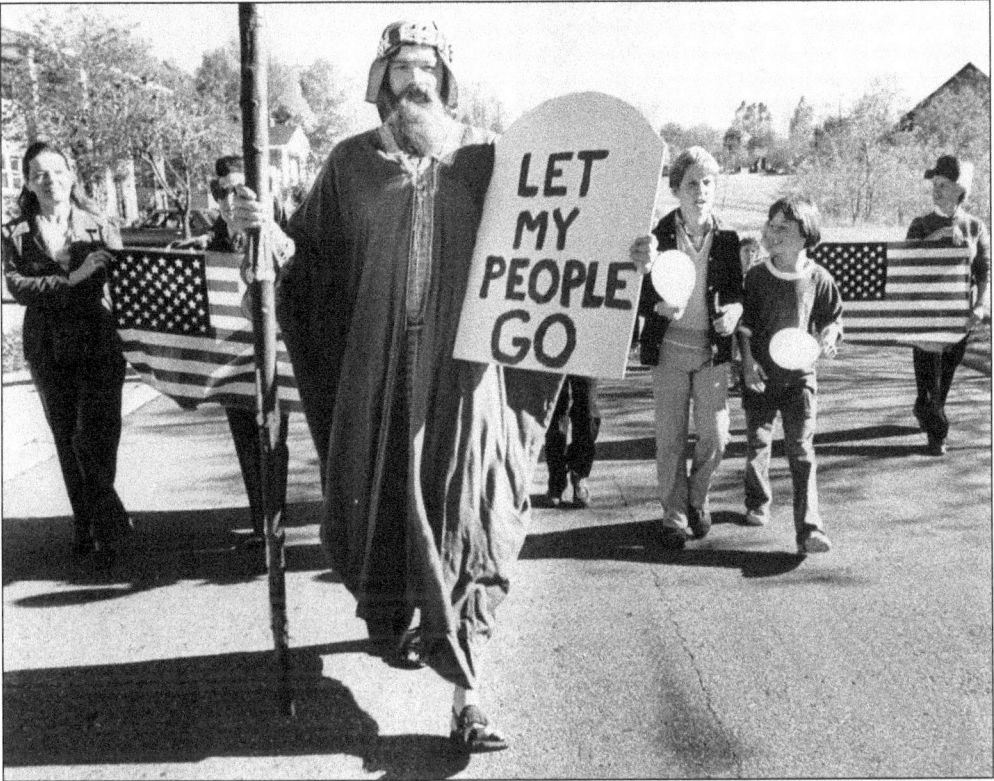

In the early 1960s, Covington annexed the then-undeveloped land, but area owners filed suit to block the annexation, and the matter lay dormant for more than two decades. In that time, the area was developed and annexed into Fort Wright. Covington then claimed ownership, and in 1980, courts ruled for Covington. A new state law, though, let Fort Wright reannex the area and put it to vote.

By November 1980, area residents led by Steve Steltenkamp held a parade urging a vote for Fort Wright. Fort Wright won by a large margin. Here resident John Eberle and Mayor Tom Litzler share a victory celebration. Litzler was mayor from 1978 to 1983, and he also served on the council and the county telecommunications board.

Judge Clyde Middleton swears in John McCormack as mayor, as Tom Jacober looks on.

This group of Fort Wright officials in the early 1980s includes, from left to right, Frank Pohlgeers, Joseph Nienaber Sr., Tom Wissel, Betty Englebeck, John McCormack, Steve Wolnitzek, and Tom Jacober.

This group of Fort Wright officials in around 1984 includes, from left to right, an unidentified local judge, Tom Jacober, Joseph Nienaber Sr., Don Martin Sr., Betty Engelman, John Schmidt, Eileen Wendt, and Tom Wissel.

This group of Fort Wright officials in around 1986 includes, from left to right, Joe Averdick, Cindy Pinto, Carl Stamm, Judge Ray Lape, Don Martin Sr., Tim Tiessen, Ken Heidrich, and Jeff Wolnitzek.

In 1988, the city purchased about 5 acres near Highland Pike and Kyles Lane to construct the current Fort Wright Municipal Building. This ground-breaking on March 2, 1990, features, from left to right, Jeff Wolnitzek, Ken Heidrich, Don Martin Sr., Tom Franxman, Cindy Pinto, and Albert Wall.

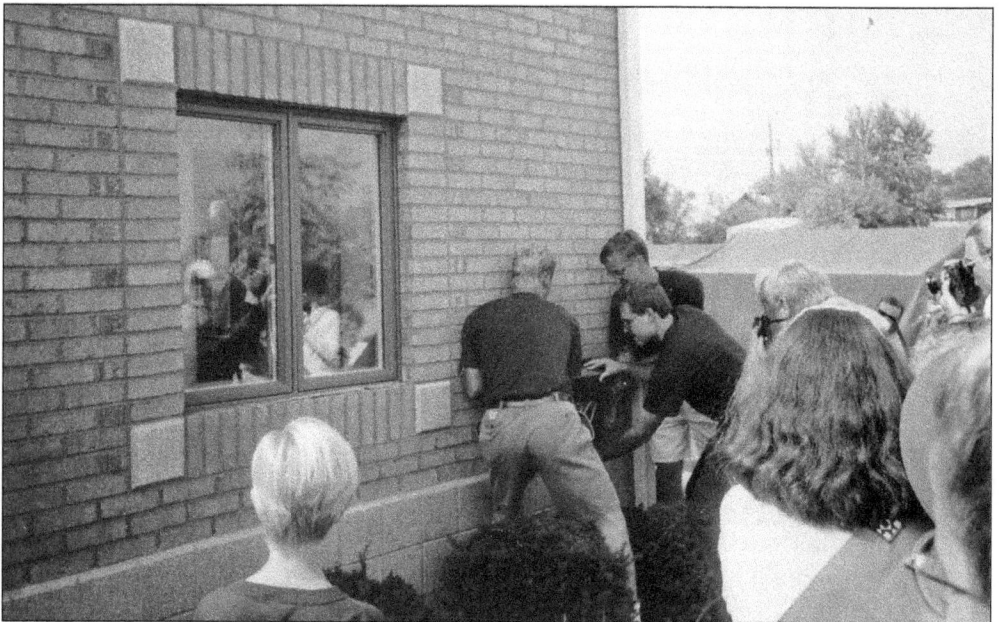

The 15,000 square feet of space in the municipal building houses the police and fire departments, all associated equipment, the city's administrative offices, and council chambers. Joseph Nienaber Jr., Don Martin Jr., and Todd Nienaber place the cornerstone at the building in 1990.

This is an aerial view of the municipal building shortly after its completion. It is situated on approximately 5 acres of land purchased for $297,000 and was ready for occupancy in November 1990.

The city's 50th anniversary was celebrated at the new building in 1991. Don Martin Sr. is speaking on the stage, and seated are, from left to right, Clyde Middleton, state representative Ken Harper, John McCormack, and George Kreutzjans Sr., the father of Fort Wright.

Neighbors turned out in large numbers at city hall to celebrate civic pride on the city's 50th anniversary. The Fort Wright Garden Club arranged publication of a historical booklet for the occasion.

After the speeches, Fort Wright held one of its traditional parades! George Kreutzjans Sr. was the parade marshal.

Six

TO PROTECT AND SERVE

In this photograph taken in 1930 at the end of Kyles Lane on Madison Pike is the first Kenton County police car. August Raterman is on the right.

The Kenton County Police Department was activated in 1918. It was once located in Fort Wright in the stone building on Dixie Highway, south of the Kuchle Garage property.

Marshals patrolled early Fort Wright using their own cars. The first marshal was Irvin Siegrist, who later became the first police chief. This 1975 photograph shows, from left to right, (first row) Assistant Chief P. Fogarty, Chief R. Myers, and Capt. G. Weaver; (second row) L. Israel, Sgt. A. Beasly, Capt. J. Murphy, Sgt. D. Catcher, D. Yocam, and B. Salle.

Pictured here in March 1978, Gene Weaver has a long record of city service. He was a Lakeview policeman, Fort Wright police captain, Fort Wright police chief, city councilman, and mayor. He served as mayor from 1999 to 2008.

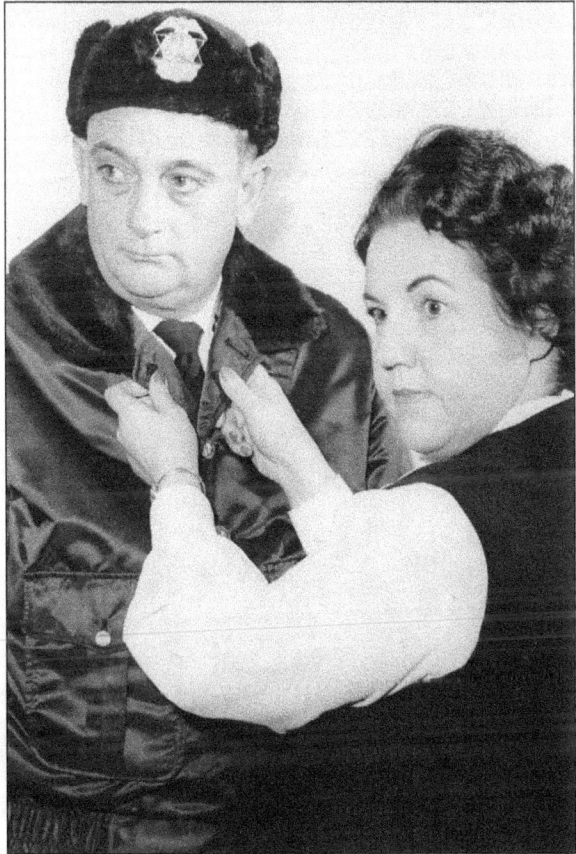

Fort Wright captain Al List, with his wife, tries on a new insulated police jacket in December 1964.

Kenton County police reserve officer Dean Russell in 1977 stands alongside a Ford Crown Victoria city cruiser. He is a city police specialist and fireman for Fort Wright and Edgewood. He served as a county deputy. Many Fort Wright children know Russell as the host of the city's bicycle safety rodeos. He volunteers as an unofficial historian and photographer for the city of Fort Wright and the Edgewood Fire Department.

The Lakeview Police Department organized in 1953, with five members under Marshal Harry Holtkamp. The officers, from left to right, are J. Eicher, A. Elam, Marshal Holtkamp, and B. Harney. Robert and Allen Elam were the only twins in Northern Kentucky police service.

Lookout Heights patrolman Charles Moore polishes his cruiser in October 1965.

A need for fire protection became apparent in Fort Wright. In 1949, the Fort Wright Civic Club (FWCC) began training about 40 men for a fire department. The club borrowed $17,000 to construct an equipment bay and buy a fire truck. Construction began in November, and in 1950, the bay, next to the civic club as shown here, became the department's home for 40 years.

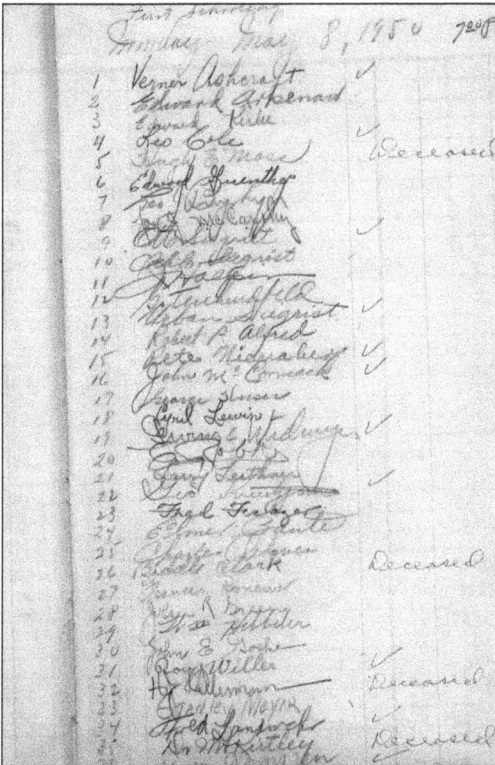

On May 8, 1950, fire volunteers signed in for an organizational meeting. Verner Ashcraft was elected the first fire chief, George Kreutzjans the assistant chief, Fred Landwehr the captain, and Henry Nienaber the lieutenant. In 1953, South Hills contracted with Fort Wright for fire protection, allowing for purchase of a second pumper. By 1955, state fire officials recognized the department as one of the best, due to the equipment and the men.

The city's first residential fire was at the home of Bob and Helen Zembrodt at 406 Kyles Lane. As seen here, the fire department then had assets of about $8,500, including 15 helmets and raincoats, hoses, and related equipment. John McCormack is one of the firefighters on the roof. McCormack was assistant fire chief for 26 years and later became councilman and then mayor from 1983 to 1984.

To raise funds for the department, a July 18–19, 1952, festival would be run by, from left to right, (kneeling) William Wartman, Fred Fraser, Bob Schabell, Currie Koch, Bob Hebbler, Otto Siegrist, and Roy Willer; (standing) Nancy Willer, Irving Widmyer, Werner Berkmeyer, Mary Ellen Deters, Pete Nienaber, Verner Ashcraft, Charles Robke, H. T. Eilerman, Dick Bogenschutz, John Luschek, L. Cole, Hugh Moss, and more.

Around 1952, Otto Siegrist, Harry Procter, and Bob Wiechman used personal station wagons for life squad calls. Women were recruited to run the squad during the day. The Ladies Auxiliary included, from left to right, Dorothy Nienaber, Ethlyn Widmyer, Kay Ross, Marian Willer, Jiffy Vonderahe, and Louise Ashcraft. The auxiliary was unusual in that the ladies both handled emergency calls and assisted on the squad.

In 1955, the firemen are, from left to right, (first row) Marshal Urban Siegrist, Mayor Irving Widmyer, Lt. John McCormack, Assistant Chief Pete Nienaber, Chief Verner Ashcraft, Assistant Chief Robert Myer, Capt. Leo Cole, Judge Roy Willer, and Robert Tranter; (second row) Fred Frazer, Edward Cooper, Otto Siegrist, Louis Johanneman, Joseph Keller, Edward Hanks, Richard McKeown, Roy Hoppenjans, and Fred Landwehr; (third row) Fred Wolnitzek, Charles Vonderahe, George Wolking, George Scheper, Richard Davidson, Robert Wiechman, Ben Roos, Robert Hebbler, and Robert Lemker.

In 1957, Chief Vern Ashcraft passed the torch of being fire chief to Pierce "Pete" Nienaber, as Fort Wright Civic Club president Ray Mueller presided.

Pete Nienaber was elected fire chief, a post he would hold 21 years, making him the city's longest-serving fire chief. The Kentucky Firemen's Association subsequently elected him president the same year, a move the front page of the *Kentucky Times Star* called an honor. He is the only Fort Wright chief to have served in that state post.

Chief Pete Nienaber is pictured with his officers. From left to right are Bob Hebbler, John McCormack, Dick Davidson, Chief Pete Nienaber, Fort Wright Civic Club president Jack Konersman, Bob Myer, and the last chief before Nienaber, Chief Vern Ashcraft.

Nienaber receives the keys to a new fire truck.

The city's fire trucks are pulled onto West Crittenden Avenue so neighbors can climb aboard.

The newspaper reported that three barns and two sheds on Harry Steenken's Highland Pike farm were destroyed in "a spectacular fire" Halloween night. The barns were ablaze when Fort Wright firemen arrived. South Fort Mitchell, Sandfordtown, and Park Hills firemen helped save the Steenken home. Firemen rescued cows, a horse, and pony. Antique wagons, stored in a barn, were destroyed. The current city building stands at this site.

Department accolades continued. In 1969, Capt. Robert Hebbler (left) accepted the state fireman of the year award from Sen. John Sherman Cooper and the Lexington fire chief. Hebbler was a three-time president of the Fort Wright Civic Club, the first basketball and baseball coach at Covington Catholic High School, and he sat 18 years on the Kenton County Election Board. His son Gary Hebbler was fire chief from 1989 until 1991.

Pictured in 1978 are, from left to right, Capt. Joe Nienaber, fire chief Bob Becker, and Capt. Charles Vonderahe. Becker was fire chief from 1978 until 1985. He became vice president of the Kentucky Firemen's Association in 1984. Joe Nienaber, one of Pete's sons, would become assistant fire chief, councilman, civic club president, the city's first city administrator, and Fort Wright mayor from 1984 to 1989. His son, Joseph Nienaber Jr., is mayor today.

Chief Bob Becker worked to modernize equipment. He is shown here with Fort Wright's 1973 Hess and Eisenhardt Cadillac ambulance. The *California Collector* featured this photograph in 2004. Retired from Fort Wright squad use in 1985, the vehicle was sold several times and used as a college football backup squad car, a Winnepeg Speedway squad car, and was an award winner at various collector car shows from 1996 through 2004.

In 1970, the city assumed financial responsibility for the fire department from the civic club in a sale of all equipment for $1. On December 8, 1990, after 40 years, the fire department physically moved from the civic club to its current 409 Kyles Lane location, housed with the city building. Also in 1990, the department hired its first full-time firefighter, and it cohosted the Kentucky Firefighters Association convention.

This team helped lead the department through the 1990s. Pictured from left to right are Daryl Tepe, Don Martin Jr., Tim Deye, Chief Ron Becker, Larry Schuler, and Doug Becker. Becker was chief from 1991 to 2001.

The fire department is pictured in 1991, the occasion of the city's 50th anniversary. The anniversary commemoration included printing a booklet of achievements. Regarding the fire department it read, in part: "For more than 50 years, your neighbors have provided a vital and sometimes dangerous service on a totally volunteer basis. . . . They are only there because they care."

The city hall veterans' memorial chronicles the service of this city to its country. From St. Agnes Parish, 103 people served in World War II. Thirty-five lived in Fort Wright, Lookout Heights, or South Hills, which comprise today's city. In this photograph, St. Agnes students surround jeeps they purchased for the war effort by saving war stamps.

Mr. and Mrs. Al Dickhaus of St. Agnes Parish had four sons in World War II. Pictured here are Edward, Robert, and Fred. Eddie was killed in action in France. Parish records show six parish members killed in action: Lt. John Wiechman, S.Sgt. Jack Kleeb, S.Sgt. Edward Dickhaus, Pfc. Fred Kluemper, Ens. Paul Bertke, and Capt. Paul Wenstrup.

This August 1960 photograph shows, from left to right, Phillip (U.S. Army), Michael, and Dennis Landwehr in front of a 1950 Mercury hardtop at 12 Kennedy Road looking up to Lake Street.

Sgt. James Louis Todtenbier of Lookout Heights died in the Vietnam War in 1969. He was the only city soldier killed in action in Vietnam.

Seven

SOCIAL, SPIRITUAL, AND SCHOOL DEVELOPMENTS

The banner of civic pride has always flown high in Fort Wright, sometimes literally. In July 1941, Odilo "Shorty" Siegrist, George Kreutzjans's brother-in-law, hitched a wagon and drove through Covington to promote Fort Wright's festival. Siegrist was instrumental in urging the postal service to establish the city's house-to-house mail service.

The South Hills Fort Wright Civic Club organized in 1939, and it evolved into the Fort Wright Civic Club. Early officers included Leo Feltel, Andy Nordmeyer, Ed Hoh, and Joe Berling. The mission was to better city conditions. In 1941, the club made a $200 donation to the city to install a traffic light at Kyles Lane and Dixie Highway. Early meetings were held in member's basements, and some early members are pictured here.

This photograph is from a civic club election flyer. Calling themselves the Progressive Ticket, pictured from left to right are (first row) Henry Nienaber, Mayor Irving Widmyer, police judge Roy Willer, and Charles Robke; (second row) Werner Berkemeyer, George Huser, Robert Tranter, and Leo Feltel. The flyer indicates that these people comprised the existing administration, which was efficient, and they were running on experience.

The membership grew too large to meet in homes. In January 1946, the club borrowed $8,500 to construct the first civic club. The first meeting in the club building was in October 1946. The civic club eventually founded the city's fire department. The club building became the site of Memorial Day programs, open houses, and more. Here Fred Wolnitzek, the city's longest-serving mayor, addresses a crowd.

Around 1955, the Fort Wright Civic Club created a baseball field on its property.

This is the 1955 civic club baseball team. Batboy Denny Wolking is in the front. From left to right are (first row) Bob Tranter, Muscles Justice, Henry Kreutzjans, Harry Ross, Joey Nienaber, Garry Justice, Al Steele, and Steve Heinen; (second row) manager Ben Ross, Bob Murray, Guy Arkenau, Dick Wolking, J. D. Bowling, Jimmy Steele, Terry McClure, Jack Martin, Tommy Hoepfner, Jimmy Deye, and coach Rudy Wolking.

The Fort Wright Civic Club underwent remodeling and expansion through the years. This included addition of a foyer, cloakroom, and kitchen, and installation of air-conditioning. Pictured from left to right, remodeling committee chairman Martin Deye, architect Mike Hargis, and committee member Mac Heidrich review blueprints for such a remodeling job.

The Fort Wright Civic Club added a floor show to its annual dinner around the 1960s. Members built the sets and performed. Bob and Alma Tranter started the follies.

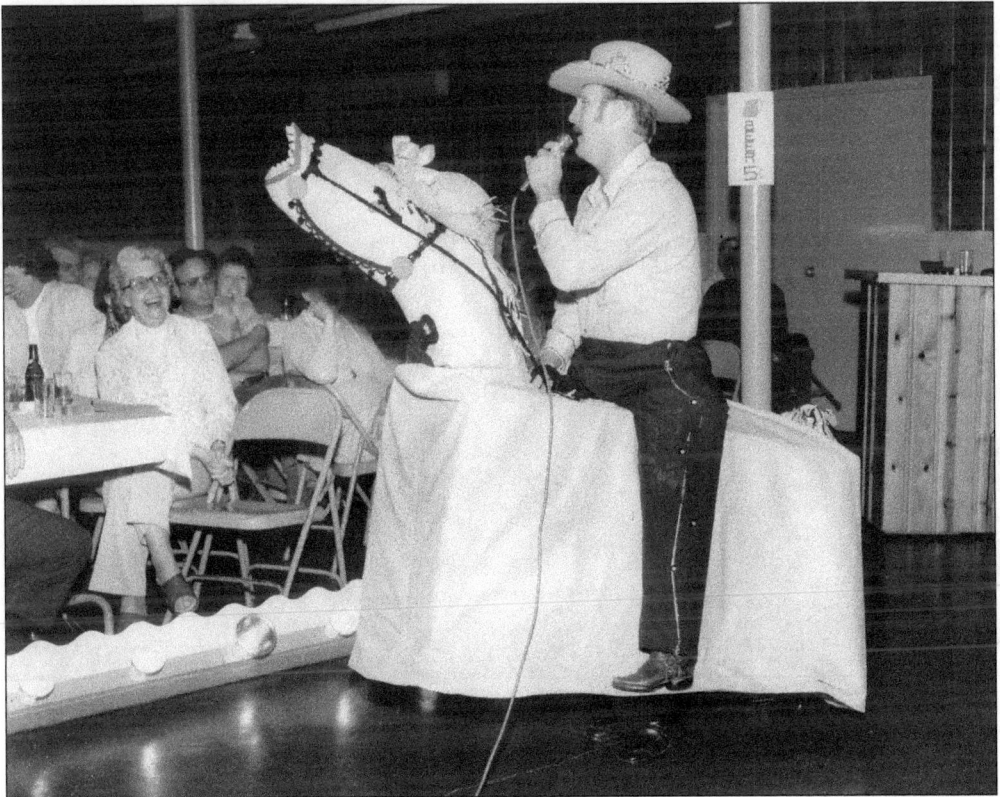

Jack Nienaber performs as the rhinestone cowboy.

Past presidents of the Fort Wright Civic Club are, from left to right, (first row) Leo Feltel (1940), Leo Brophy (1941), Vice Pres. John Goeke, Roger Kathmann (1944), and Vince Minogue (1961 and 1979); (second row) George Rudy Wolking (1942), Irving Widmyer (1946 and 1947), and Bob Tranter (1954); (third row) Mac Heidrich (1974), Mike Barnes (1977), Dick McKeown (1957), Walt Behler (1971), Ron Nienaber (1972), John McCormack (1949), Bob Hebbler (1952, 1953, and 1963),

Andy Nordmeyer (1958), Ed Hanks (1955), Ray Schuler (1970), and Ruth Schuler (1978); (fourth row) Frank Wolnitzek (1968 and 1969), Don Martin (1964), Ray Mueller (1956), Jack Konersman (1960), Joseph Nienaber Sr. (1973), Bob Becker (1975 and 1976), Walt Schomaker (1965), Joe Summe (1959), and Bob Wiechman (1962).

Eventually, Fort Wright would expand its boundaries, taking in the communities of South Hills in 1960, Lookout Heights in 1968, and Lakeview in 1978. The 1966 Lookout Heights Civic Club officers are, from left to right, (first row) secretary Norma Moore and treasurer John Herold; (second row) second vice president Jim Schilling, Pres. John Enwright, and first vice president Vince Melching.

In 1961, Bluegrass Swim Club opened in Fort Wright as a private membership swimming facility. South Hills trustee and Bluegrass Swim Club charter member Ed Stutler made movies of the pool's construction and opening. One group of officers is pictured here. From left to right are Michele Brucato, Mrs. Robert Oehler, Mrs. Robert Niemeyer, and Mrs. Norbert Saalfeld.

July 4, 1993, was so hot that when they called for adult swim at Bluegrass Swim Club, the adults actually got in the water. Kids between 6 and 18 were not allowed in the pool at this time, and kids under 6 had to be accompanied by an adult. Normally adult swim time finds only a handful of people in the pool.

Molly Gleeson, age seven, and Annie Meyers, age nine, float in a rubber raft in 1981 at the Bluegrass Swim Club. Bluegrass is a member of the Northern Kentucky Swim League (NKSL), which, in 2009, is in its 46th season, according to the *Kentucky Enquirer*.

This is a photograph of the 1969 Bluegrass Swim Club swim and dive team. The team won the Northern Kentucky Swim League (NKSL) A League Championship.

In August 1930, Msgr. Gerard Geisen called the Sisters of Notre Dame. He said the diocese was opening a school September 1, 1930, that they wanted the sisters to operate. He added that a portable church would be erected by October, though neither was started. Sr. Mary Angela noted time was short. Monsignor said they could manage their part if she could manage hers. She did. Church records say St. Agnes Church began.

The Knochelmans donated several acres of Lookout Heights ground and $10,000 to build the chapel, according to a 1930 *Kentucky Post*. The parish purchased the balance of the 11-acre site. The chapel was from Sears and Roebuck. The bell was donated from the Twelfth Street firehouse in Covington. The chapel remained an annex of the Cathedral Parish until 1954, when St. Agnes received parish status.

The first Mass in the St. Agnes Chapel was celebrated on October 5, 1930. In 1936, St. Agnes Chapel was host to the double wedding of Freida Kuchle and Bob Hais, and Rose Kuchle and Bill Avery. By 2005, more than 2,000 couples had married at St. Agnes.

In 1931, the *Kentucky Post* reported the chapel had grown to 125 families, with 45 pupils in school. By 1938, the congregation had outgrown the chapel and plans were made to build a larger chapel. Bishop Howard laid the cornerstone of the new chapel on May 22, 1938.

The resulting church looks much as St. Agnes stands today, a landmark on the city's horizon. The church pastors have been Rev. Msgr. Charles Towell (1954–1971), Msgr. Ed Hickey (1971–1982), Msgr. John Murphy (1982–1992), Rev. Msgr. Donald Hellman (1992–1999), and Rev. Mark Keene, who began his service in 1999.

This 1959 interior shot shows Monsignor Towell wearing a miter, a privilege he had as protonotary apostolic. The pews are along the side of the walls. The pews were replaced in 1961, and the old pews were sent to Mary Queen of Heaven Church. There are no stained-glass windows. Those were installed between 1960 and 1963, before the annex was built.

This photograph, from around 1959, again shows pews attached to the walls. The first parish council was established in June 1969 and included John O'Hara, Robert Dickman, Dr. Carl Brueggemann, Charles Hanneken, Walter Behler, George Kreutzjans, Charles Mayleben, and Joe Gausepohl.

St. Agnes Parish began its music ministry with the men and boys' choir in the early 1950s.

The faith community continued to grow in Fort Wright. On June 15, 1967, Rev. Arthur Little reported on the building of the Central Church of the Nazarene.

In February 1979, pictured from left to right, (first row) Leslie Roth, Betty Klette, Audrey Jackson, and Virginia Wedding join (second row) Rev. William Jones and Martin Roberts to plan the dedication of St. Paul United Church of Christ in Fort Wright.

Fort Wright is home to Fort Wright Elementary and St. Agnes School. The old Knochelman homestead was converted in 1930 to St. Agnes Chapel School. Enrollment grew so rapidly that grades five through eight met at St. Joseph Heights from 1932 to 1939, returning when the new church was built. The first school board included principal Sister Edwardine, Walter Behler, John O'Hara, Harold McKinley, Lawrence Emark, and Bill Sommerkamp.

The 1931 first communion class is pictured with Msgr. Gerhard Geisen in front of the frame chapel. By 2005, more than 4,700 people had made their first communion at the parish.

This 1937 first communion class includes, from left to right, (first row) Martha Rose Schnorbus, Mary Catherine Schuler, Fr. Joseph Collins, Nancy Lee Oelsner, and Vivian Schepard; (second row) Richard Hubbard, Veva May Schnorbus, Carol with unknown surname, Virginia Schuler, Tessie Court, Mary Jean Court, Marilyn Shepard, and Jerry Finke; (third row) Eugene Febry, Ralph Kuchle, Jimmy Bauer, Joseph with unknown surname, Susan Jane Eilerman, Bobby Schmidt, Maurice Murphy, Jack Flack, and Frank Schulte.

This is a St. Agnes School class photograph from 1941.

The St. Agnes Holy Name baseball team poses in approximately 1940.

A group of St. Agnes School students stands in front of the buses in the 1950s.

In 1959, St. Agnes Boy Scout Troop No. 31 rides in their float in the Holy Name Parade. The float is passing the Kresge Five and Dime on Madison Avenue in Covington.

From 1959 to 1978, Kentucky closed the public kindergarten system. In response to this community need, Betty White operated Fort Wright's first private kindergarten for those 19 years. Her school was in her West Henry Clay home and a cumulative 450 children attended classes. This is White's 1966 kindergarten class. Mille Fangman subsequently operated a private kindergarten in St. Paul's Church in Fort Wright until the early 1980s.

Betty White's first kindergarten class of 1960 includes, from left to right, (first row) Chris Radamacher, Mary Flottman, Jeanette Helmer, Miriam Gehring, Jane White, Cathy Holthaus, and Billy VanSant; (second row) Sharon Hebbler, Mary Rose Lindemann, Randy Lemker, Gayle Pille, David Gray, Stephen Meier, Jeffrey Hinchy, Judy Meihaus, and Margaret Steenken; (third row) Mimi Zumbiel, Gary Goetz, David Borchers, Barbara Hanneken, Burke Price, Bobby Kenning, Cathy Dickman, Danny Miller, and JoAnn White.

In 1984, Judy Gilliam came and started St. Agnes kindergarten after piloting the return of public kindergartens to Kenton County schools. She taught Fort Wright kindergartners for 21 years, was recognized as the *Kentucky Post* Teacher of the Year, and became assistant principal. Her daughter, Stacey Turner, became the kindergarten teacher in 2005, was the 2008 Reds Teacher of the Year, and was named a Kentucky Colonel for teaching.

Eight

NEIGHBORS HELPING NEIGHBORS

Fort Wright has something special—its people. In 1948, Joseph and Josephine Kuchle celebrated their 50th wedding anniversary with a Mass at St. Agnes. They arrived in horse and buggy. The children raised at the Kyles Lane and Dixie highway homestead included Carl (1900), Bertha (1901), Joseph Jr. (1902), Ursula (1903), Helen (1905), Alice (1907), JoAnn (1909), Marie (1910), Emily (1911), Freida (1913), Ruth and Rose (1914), and John (1915).

The Knochelman matriarchs are pictured in the 1900s. From left to right are (first row) Julia, Grandma Rose, and Christine; (second row) Theresa, Rose, and Beine. Their farm was off of Kyles Lane. The Knochelmans bought their farm from Robert Samuel Kyle, for whom Kyle's Lane is named.

Christine and a friend pick daisies on the Knochelman farm.

Fred Landwehr and Rosemary Schwer were married in June 1937 at the farm at Kyles Lane and Highland Avenue. They were early members of the Madison Avenue Hog Angels, Harley-Davidson riders who helped distressed motorists. They owned Landwehr Hardware in Covington and Fred was the Fort Wright Fire Department's first captain. They raised their three sons on Kennedy Road in Fort Wright.

Bud Tenhunfeld and children plant a tree on West Crittenden Avenue around 1947.

In 1948, Mary and Alvin Appel were married at St. Agnes Church.

The sons of fire chief Pete and his wife, Dorothy Nienaber, are, from left to right, (first row) Bill and Joseph; (second row) Jack and Pierce Nienaber, around 1950. The brothers were raised at 37 West Crittenden Avenue. That home and the Barbara Circle home of Henry Nienaber, Pete's brother, have been Nienaber homes since construction. Two of the brothers, five of their children, and 11 grandchildren reside in Fort Wright today.

The Lou Johanneman family is pictured near Kyles Lane, behind today's Frisch's, around 1953.

The Foltz family is pictured around 1954.

Pictured from left to right in 1959, Patty (7), JoAnn (5), and Jane (3) White grew up at 11 West Henry Clay, the daughters of Allan and Betty White. Allan White is well known across the region for his work in Cincinnati television.

Fred and Judy Fischer are part of Fort Wright's fabric. Married September 5, 1959, they moved to Fort Wright and raised Joe, Cammie, Tricia, Chris, Missy, Tony, and Sarah. They were charter members of Bluegrass Swim Club, the Fort Wright and South Hills Civic Clubs, and St. Agnes. Several of their children have established their families in Fort Wright.

Steve and Judy Gilliam raised Stephanie, Stacey, and Jan in Park Hills and Fort Wright. Steve was on the board of Bluegrass Swim Club for 15 years, starting his service at the time of the pool's construction in around 1960.

Mrs. Odile Siegrist, Laureen Siegrist (5), and Mrs. Charles Stoess sit on a Fort Wright porch step in June 1965 helping Laureen read.

In a 1966 story by Chester Geaslen picked up by the Associated Press, the *Kentucky Post* featured these Ridgemont Avenue "backyard battlers." Jeff Carroll (eight) and David Warning (eight) of Ridgemont and Joe Fischer (six) of Fayette Avenue climbed trees, hid in garbage cans, and took cover behind stones. Buzz Rischell (six) and Dan Warning (six) were also pictured.

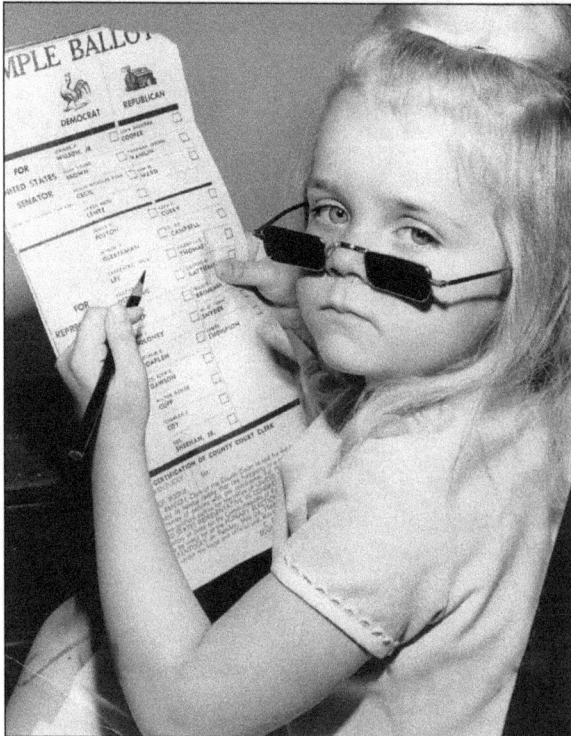

Euteine "Teena" Smith (five) of Fort Wright surveys a 1966 sample ballot.

120

Fort Wright's George Jr. and Geraldine Kreutzjans were the 1967 king and queen of the Catholic Kolping Society of Cincinnati ball. Their court included Rudy and Margaret Eismann, George and Brune Gerdes, and Nick and Marie Kreutzjans, all of Lookout Heights, and John and Helen Fincken, Bill and Chris Janszen, George and Barbara Kreutzjans, Rudy and Angela Pholabeln, Ed and Marty Pohlgeers, and Joe and Mary Vormbrocke, all of Fort Wright.

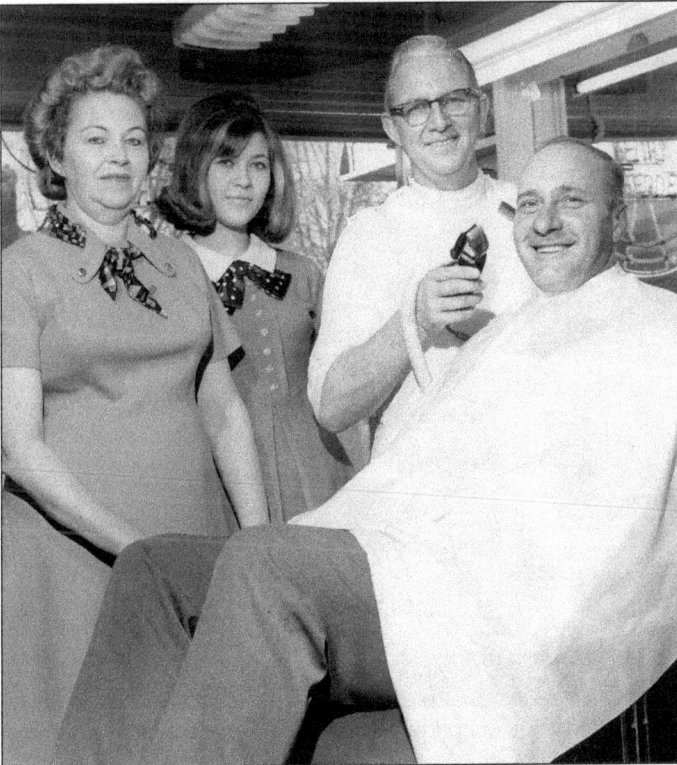

Fort Wright barber Henry Scherder prepares to cut the hair of Elsmere mayor Leo Brun in 1969, while Mrs. Leo Brun and Rose Mary look on.

Fort Wright's Richard Rolfsen was elected president of the Kentucky Pharmaceutical Association in 1971. He and his family resided on Edna Lane.

The Wolnitzek brothers met in the early 1970s with Kentucky governor Wendell Ford. Pictured from left to right are Fred, Frank, Jack, Gov. Wendell Ford, Bob, and George. The Wolnitzek brothers were business and government leaders at the city, county, and state levels. A Wolnitzek was mayor or on Fort Wright council in part of every decade since at least 1960.

Fort Wright's Frank Wolnitzek was a well-known restaurant owner and civic activist. Fort Wright families equate his Chef Barone's to homemade pizza packs. He served two terms on council, was a fire and life squad volunteer, and civic club president. His son Jeff Wolnitzek also served on council.

Nick and Cyrilla Brake of Fort Wright are pictured in 1978. He served as president of Lookout Heights Civic Club. She was manager at the St. Agnes cafeteria.

Fort Wright's Garry and Joyce Edmondson await election results. Garry Edmondson served on city council. He has been the Kenton County attorney since 1993. His office prosecutes 80,000 cases a year, and he was named the Kentucky County Attorney of the Year for 1997–1998.

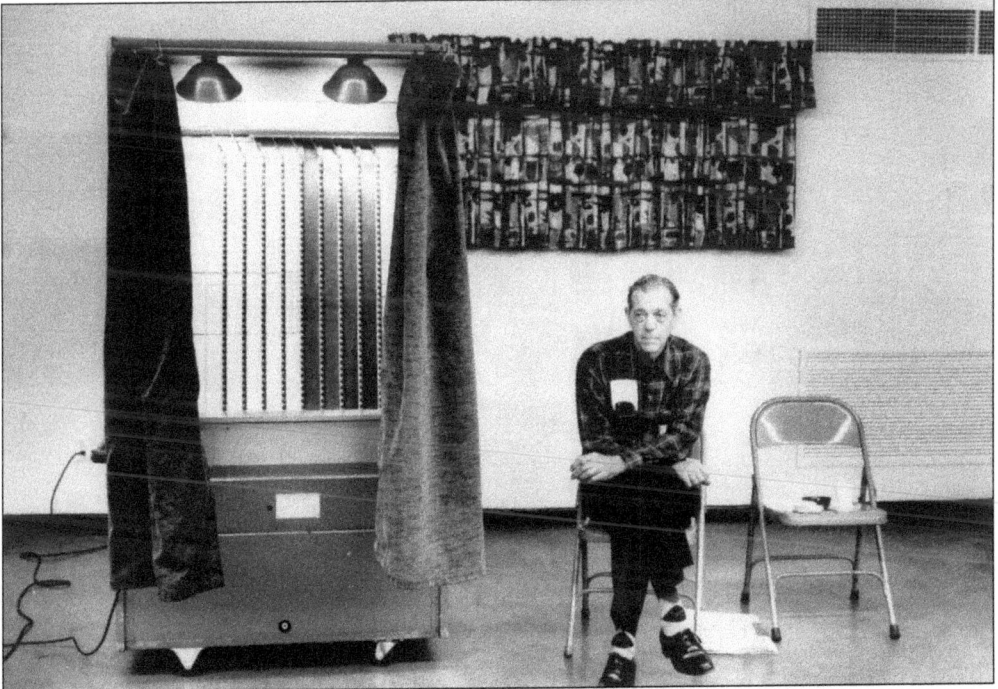

Fort Wright election judge Lester Miller waits for voters in 1979.

Pictured in the 1980s are, from left to right, Fort Wright's Shannon, Joseph, Marianne, Dr. Kevin, Albert "Bert," and Scott Wall. Bert was in the elite 3rd U.S. Infantry Guard in the early 1960s, and he marched in John F. Kennedy's inaugural parade. He served on city council and in the fire department. His son Scott now serves on city council.

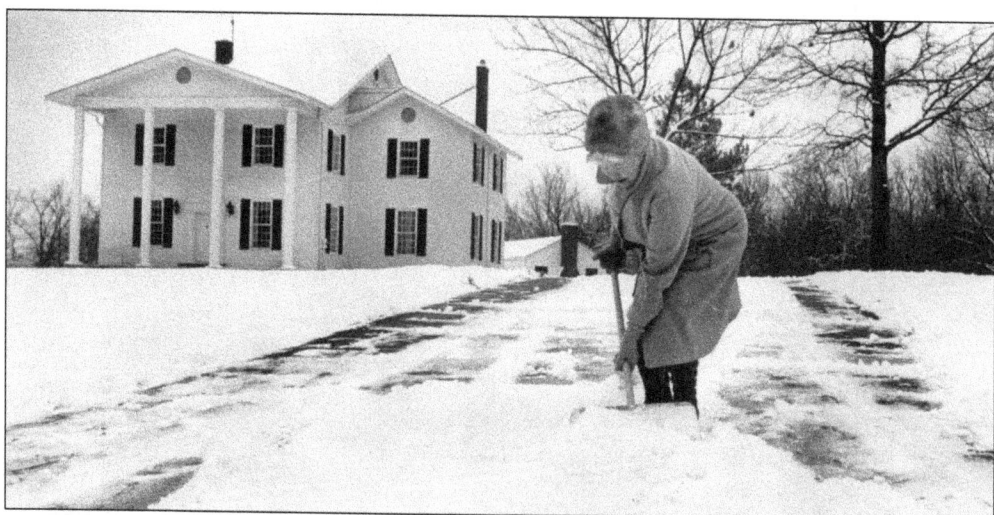

Longtime Fort Wright resident Norma Bonnett shovels her drive of snow at 3339 Madison Pike in 1982. In earlier years, a pay-to-fish lake was located on this section of 3-L Highway. The Bonnet home was sold and today the building houses a veterinary hospital.

Tracing their Fort Wright family history back to the Civil War, Don Sr. and Anita Martin raised their children, pictured here, from left to right, around 1970, Nancy, Steve, Don, Jenny, and Marianne "Murph" on Barbara Circle in Fort Wright. The Martins have a collective family history of military and fire service. Don Jr. was a fireman for 18 years and served on city council, and Marianne's husband, Joe Averdick, is currently on the council.

Luvenia Haughabod, a Fort Wright grandmother of five, asks a question during a 1989 town hall meeting hosted by city police.

Visit us at
arcadiapublishing.com

www.ingramcontent.com/pod-product-compliance
Lightning Source LLC
Chambersburg PA
CBHW050622110426
42813CB00007B/1687